MANAGING LIBRARY SERVICES FOR CHILDREN AND YOUNG PEOPLE

a practical handbook

MANAGING LIBRARY SERVICES FOR CHILDREN AND YOUNG PEOPLE

a practical handbook

Catherine Blanshard

Head of Leeds Library and Information Services
Leeds Leisure Services

LIBRARY ASSOCIATION PUBLISHING
LONDON

© Catherine Blanshard 1998

Published by
Library Association Publishing
7 Ridgmount Street
London WC1E 7AE

Library Association Publishing is wholly owned by The Library Association.

First published 1998

British Library Cataloguing in Publication Data

A catalogue record for this book is available from the British Library.

ISBN 1-85604-226-X

Typeset in 11/14pt Aldine 721 BT and Zurich by Library Association Publishing.
Printed and made in Great Britain by Bookcraft (Bath) Ltd, Midsomer Norton, Somerset.

Contents

Dedication

Thanks to Robbie Macpherson who inspired me to learn new management techniques and to Ann Parker for first introducing me to the magic of children's librarianship. Thanks also to Sue Jones, Helen Boothroyd, to all young people's specialists and especially to the staff both of Hertfordshire's Schools Library Service and of their public library service, who give kids a great deal every day.

Acknowledgments

Quotations from well-known children's books have been given by kind permission of the authors, to whom I owe a particular debt for giving children and librarians such riches with which to work. Quotations from education, business, social observation and library texts have again been reproduced with the kind permission of the authors. Thanks are also due to the library authorities who sent in their material for inclusion in this book and to Alec Williams of Leeds Library Service, who helped me to look into the future.

Preface

> She's off libraries . . . Like everyone else, she had this rosy vision of
> libraries as cool and silent repositories of neatly-shelved wisdom: temples
> of learning, gems of culture, high-points of civilisation, that sort of thing.
> If I said I was going to the library, she'd smile and go all soft inside.
>
> A. Fine, *Goggle-eyes*[1]

Throughout the world, where a public library service exists, there have
been fundamental shifts in both local and national provision. The
changes that surround library services are unpredictable and affect
everything from the broad social structure of the community they serve,
through the needs and expectations of that community, to the management, financial structure and organization of the individual library
authority.

This change undoubtedly reflects the change in lifestyles, needs and
expectations of citizens in many parts of the world. Greater desire for
knowledge and for access to information, new demands for an individual's rights to be recognized and not least the revolution in technology
make the services of the library even more vital than before. All of this
is being seen in increased use and changing demand. Libraries are, however, in most places, institutions that were built around books, and some
citizens have the perception that they are unable to change enough to
adequately meet their broadening needs. Others have disregarded the
library, often without investigating it, because it is not 'new' enough and
therefore it is assumed not to be relevant to them. The fundamental role
of libraries in information provision is not understood by those who
think that the information needs of society are a new concept – a new
industry to be marketed.

As a result of these huge changes in society and of the lack of recognition of the fact that libraries have altered in any way, the future for the
profession might be assessed as bleak. Libraries could be passed by. If
they are, it will be the fault of the profession, and society will lose an

important keystone in its fabric.

The Comedia report *Libraries in a world of cultural change*[2] (1995) identified some of the roles that the library plays in the community. It put forward the concept of the library as a home within a public place, providing an 'entry point to a wider society for many different groups'. The library is a source of vitality and a focus to both urban and rural areas. It is the citizens' free access point to knowledge. It offers a relatively safe place for children to be in this less than safe world, and the library ticket is described as 'likely to be one of the child's first links to a wider society and one of the first ways of being recognised as an individual citizen'.

Libraries need to change. They must be more flexible, less hierarchical, less protective of the 'professional mystique'. They need to be focused, process-oriented and in touch with the needs and desires of both users and non-users. They need to know what they are trying to achieve, what they want to be. Libraries, whether autonomous or part of a wider organization, need clear strategies, objectives, implementation plans and a system of evaluation to ensure that they achieve their stated purpose. In short, they need to adopt new management techniques and learn from successful business practices.

As the Comedia report said, 'it therefore becomes imperative that the public library movement urgently promotes a more dynamic image of itself, cultivates opinion formers among the younger generation and proclaims its cultural modernism with pride rather than defensiveness and evasion.' The writers of the Comedia report studied library services in depth. They concluded that the majority of libraries are not sufficiently aware of the significance of changes happening in society, nor are they responding to them.

This view has been picked up by the Audit Commission, whose report *Due for renewal* (1997)[3] again urges libraries to change, and to develop a costing, stock, training and strategic process to aid them in this. *New library: the people's network* (1997)[4] meanwhile gives an excellent charter for change with many valuable recommendations.

Over the last few years children's services across the UK, Europe, Australia and the USA have begun to rise to the challenge of change. Management styles and structures have changed, and involvement in cross-service and multi-agency working has brought new opportunities in service provision and greater recognition by budget holders. It has not all been easy: there have been losses, some traditional approaches have been sacrificed, status has been hit. There have also been many successes. The aim of this book is to share the ways in which library services have risen to the challenge; how they have changed or adapted their management style and their principles, and how they have repackaged their products. From the experiences of those services that have made such changes, a few common and fundamental principles for success can be drawn.

The children's library service of the future will:

- have a clear knowledge of the aims of every element of its provision, building to a strong sense of purpose;
- have clear values and goals;
- continually reassess its services, measuring performance and evaluating results;
- plan strategies for every aspect of the service, including how it will be provided;
- communicate with its users, ensuring they play a key role in service development.

As a result, the children's service will attract partners who are keen to work with libraries, who understand why libraries are crucial to them. It will also attract sponsorship in kind and money, enabling developments, innovations and access to be available for all. Most important of all, it will give children and young people a service they need and want for their future.

With this high level of interest and potential for the children's service, it is appropriate to take a fresh look at how we lead and manage provision. We can learn from the best practice of business and public sectors, and focus provision on users. This book aims to show that if we know what we are doing and how we are doing it and organize around the child, the future is bright.

The introduction aims to set the scene and look at how children's services arrived at their current situation. The book is then divided into four parts. Part 1 outlines the management techniques required for the children's library business to survive and grow in this time of rapid change. This first section begins by helping to identify the point that a library or whole service has reached, what it is trying to achieve, and how it must change to achieve its ultimate aim. The book explains some of the techniques which can provide the means to bring about change, such as SWOT – analysing strengths, weaknesses, opportunities and threats – and STEP – analysing social, technological, economic and political implications – analysis, product lifestyles, force field analysis and marketing.

Part 1 then introduces a simple 'model of organizational performance' which may be used for all aspects of service development and can become an invaluable tool in planning. The aim or purpose of the service is defined, and objectives are set, including the desired features and benefits of the service, and there is a comprehensive investigation of the users.

Having developed a full explanation of the purposes of the library, the book moves on to investigate the management of the service. Issues of leadership, values, time management, staff performance management and benchmarking are discussed. Part 1 then closes with an investigation of quality issues and advises how to demonstrate the value the children's service adds to the public library service as a whole and to the lives of children.

Following development of the theme of management framework in Part 1, Part 2 outlines approaches to the development of the strategies needed to deliver such a crucial service. This section provides a detailed breakdown of the activities underpinning services to under-fives, children and young people, including special needs provision, activities, IT use, budgeting, sponsorship and stock.

Part 3 investigates the three topical issues of children's services today: literacy, educational trends and partnership working. The literacy standards and activities of children have been under the spotlight for many years but are now under intense investigation. Support for parents, additional schooling and fun, imaginative projects are all being developed to help. These sometimes conflict with and sometimes support current educational developments. The role of the community in learning is in conflict with the somewhat rigid National Curriculum and its equivalent in Scotland and elsewhere. These developments create a huge opportunity for the children's library service to develop a crucial role. Working in partnership with others will give even more opportunities and possible sources of finance to develop new services and fine tune old ones to meet the growing demands of today's young people.

Part 4, the final section of the book, looks to the future and raises some of the issues which services continue to face. If they use the model outlined in Part 1, individual libraries and library authorities should be in great shape to face what is an uncertain but challenging time ahead. This section of the book demonstrates how the profession can benefit from management techniques developed by business; how these do not necessarily threaten the basis of provision but, on the contrary, can strengthen it by providing strong and often irrefutable arguments for the need for children's services. Such an attitude will encourage libraries to positively let go of some aspects of service and look at how to repackage others to fit better into the ever-changing world. Once the skills required to do this have been learnt, provision can be repackaged and refocused rapidly and with ease with every ensuing new user need.

This book aims to be of use not only to those readers who are currently responsible for a children's section in a library and who would like to take a fresh look at the services they offer, but also to those new to managing a structured group of libraries or a whole authority service. For these readers, it offers ideas and experience from others and new ways of looking at services. The importance of clear aims and objectives, plans for implementation, and clear evaluation are crucial to effectiveness in times of diminishing resources. For those readers who are managing a group of libraries or a whole authority the book offers a strategic approach to provision. The development of strategies, policies and guidelines for the whole service, combined with monitoring and evaluation, provides arguments for funding, and service development. This approach will allow you to grasp opportunities and enable you to demonstrate to those in other departments, to elected members and to the chief executive why your service is so important to them. If after reading it you feel you would like to share your experiences of developing your service, or if you have more ideas to share, then the intention is to make this book come alive – to make it interactive. Wherever in the world you might be, if you have access to the Internet then you can add to the ideas in the book, share your experiences and chat to colleagues. The aim is to create a worldwide living professional development site for children's library services over the ether of the superhighway. This site is currently being created by the Association of Senior Children's and Educational Librarians (ASCEL).

If you are not a technical addict, don't worry! You can e-mail your ideas to me at <catherine.blanshard@leeds.gov.uk> and I will put them on the children's library service home page – or why not ask a colleague who has Internet access? The Library Association also has a Web site for you to contact. The address is www.la-hq.org.uk. Alternatively if you want to read developments in hard copy then, in the UK, ASCEL will continue to produce its Newsletter and guide sheets, which will summarize what is appearing on the Internet. They welcome members from around the world.

Outside the UK, try your own country's national library organization, or if that is not available, and you don't feel like starting one, then join the International Federation of Library Associations (IFLA) or International Board on Books for Young People (IBBY) and keep up to date through journals.

References

1   Fine, A., *Goggle-eyes*. Harmondsworth, Penguin, 1989.
2   Greenhalgh, L. and Worpole, K. with Landry, C., *Libraries in a world of cultural change*, London, UCL Press, 1995.
3   Audit Commission, *Due for renewal*, 1997, Audit Commission Office.
4   Library and Information Commission, *New library: the people's network*, October 1997. LIC, 2 Sheraton Street, London W1V 4BH.

Introduction

Change is not new. It has been on the agenda of management teams for many years and it *is* now the agenda. This is certainly true of children's library services. Back in 1985 in the UK the key providers of children's services across the country got together to discuss the state of children's services. They titled this work *Crisis or challenge – the future of library services to children and young people*.[1, 2]

Children's professionals of the day felt the service was being squeezed. Not only was there increasing demand resulting from the great success of teenage publishing and the beginning of 'series' publishing for younger readers, but also, and perhaps more significantly, there was immense pressure from professionals in other sectors of public librarianship.

The children's librarian was equated with 'cut and paste' activities which were seen as frivolous, costly, time-consuming and noisy, making a mess and disturbing the grown-ups. Downgrading of the specialism resulted, and the 'specialist versus generalist' debate gathered momentum. Children's literature and librarianship courses were also removed from many university and college curriculums, and it is only the determination and dedication of people like Professor Judith Elkin, Head of the School of Information Studies, University of Central England in Birmingham, which have kept children's librarianship on the syllabus at all.

The Library and Information Services Council (LISC) unwittingly aggravated the situation in producing *School libraries: the foundations of the curriculum*.[3] This excellent report focused the attention of the profession on meeting the library needs of the child through the school. While the report did a great deal of good in that sphere, some chief librarians used it as an excuse to underfund, or ignore, children's public library services, not recognizing that they met very different needs from those met by the school library.

So *Crisis or challenge* was born, and it produced some stunning proposals clearly ahead of its time. The heads of service who got together to tackle the situation saw these as the key issues:[1, 2]

- Library services to children and young people are at a crossroads. The only certainty is that services are changing and we must learn to manage that change or find the specialism totally subordinated.
- Courses in children's work at library schools are already scarce.
- Changing emphasis in services, and management and administrative structures, have led to a diminution and dilution of specialist work.

They went on to pose a series of questions going to the very heart of children's librarianship:

- Do we know what is the major purpose of children's work?
- What direction is it taking?
- What services are special to the children's field?
- Do we know what are our priorities? What is the most effective use of time and resources?
- Should we define core and peripheral activities?
- Should we redefine the needs of children to take account of their quicker maturation, other interests, education, shopping patterns and so on?
- Can we improve the library image?

What happened to this challenging thinking? On the one hand, because it sounds so fresh and relevant to today's situation, it does not seem that long ago. In that time however, world developments have been phenomenal: we have had the introduction of fax machines, interactive technology and word processing; the fall of Communism in what was the Eastern bloc, the unification of Germany and the end of apartheid in South Africa.

If the issues raised by *Crisis or challenge* are still relevant, why has it taken so long to respond to them and to implement change? The answer seems to be that *Crisis or challenge* prompted ten years of protectionism and defence of the children's library service position, alienating a number of senior managers in the process. This took the form of attempts to maintain the status quo and a great deal of energy was expended in demanding a LISC report on children's libraries.

Behind the scenes, however, the metamorphosis of the service was taking place and so, when the environment began to change and children went back to the top of the political agenda, children's library services throughout the world were ready to take advantage. A number of countries have focused on children's rights and needs, and, as a result, a different approach to children's library service management has evolved. Customer care, targeting services to customer groups, delegation of responsibility, teamwork, measuring and managing performance, evaluating success and assessing the value added by service provision have all become fashionable in business and in politics. These are the principles behind the questions posed in *Crisis or challenge*. Those individuals and services who had been working to direct their provision in line with these principles suddenly found the environment right for them to do so.

Australia and a few European countries, such as Denmark and Greece, for example, have made great developments in children's librarianship. In the UK, legislation such as the Children Act[4] broke new ground in recognizing that children need better care and have certain legal rights. It made stringent demands on authorities who supported children to improve their provision. Meanwhile the Education Act[5] had already introduced business practices into education with local management of schools. More recently there has been a national focus on librarianship. Documents such as *The review of the public library service in England and Wales*,[6] the Department of National Heritage (DNH) *Contracting-out in public libraries*[7] and *Reading the future* (DNH)[8] have all brought the gaze of government onto librarianship in general. Two government publications, *School library services and financial delegation*[9] and *Investing in children*[10] made the focus on children's work quite intense.

Investing in children is in fact the report *Crisis or challenge* called for ten years previously. While the wait was long and painful, its impact is all the more great for its timing. The awareness raised by the Children Act and Education Act and the growing concern for children has meant that the persuasive and focused recommendations of *Investing in children* have been acted upon by government both locally and nationally. There has been acceptance of the fundamental role children have within the whole public library service across the UK. Admittedly it is grudging in some places, and still to permeate all parts, but the evidence of a change of attitude is strong. To ensure that this happens, *Reading the future* says 'Library Authorities will be required to set out their charter for children's services in their annual Public Library Plan'. The Library and Information Commission in *2020 vision*[11] proposed that we should 'empower the individual by providing resources and information for particular groups, especially children and young people, and facilitating the development of the information skills which are essential for modern-day living'. This is the only group of users of any library service which is specified in the whole document. These statements have been invaluable, and, when they are read alongside the Comedia Report,[12] prove that children's librarianship is of great relevance today.

This work has provided a catalyst for change and has enabled the children's specialists to dispense with the defensive approach and to demonstrate what has been achieved. In many countries, by working together across political and geographical boundaries, the children's service has raised itself to a new level. European Union projects, such as Lancashire's Bookevent, have broadened children's horizons. Cross agency working between libraries, social services, education departments and voluntary groups to support the information needs of very young children and their carers is another excellent example of change.

Many children's services throughout the UK have taken on the challenge of the above-mentioned reports and are responding to their recommendations. What we need to do globally to really take advantage of the situation is to stand back and take a look at how to re-invent children's services. We have the opportunity to take advantage of the focus on children. We must not get caught up in 'tradition', in 'principles' and in 'professionalism' if they are inappropriate to young people's needs. This does not mean that we should throw the baby out with the bath water, but equally we should not let the past get in the way of the future. A framework needs to be provided for the service so that it can be accountable to users, understood both by the elected representatives or paymasters and by senior management teams and given full commitment by staff. Children's library professionals must look at the big picture and re-invent provision so that we can truly 'invest in children' to give them what they want and need.

Moreover, as the budget of the public library is squeezed, children's work has the potential to attract money to a library authority. It is often the area where sponsorship is to be found, and where joint working is possible. The children's service can be easily linked to the education and social agenda of the day, and so elected representatives or paymasters can gain some high profile 'quick wins' which can enhance their political position. Being politically aware of the implications of decisions, and using this knowledge to the advantage of the service, is where success lies. Unfortunately this is not a skill which comes easily to librarians.

The needs of children and young people are fundamental to the development of any nation. A children's library is a core part of this, so it is necessary for children's library professionals to specifically relate children's provision to the current agenda. They must be politically astute enough to use the jargon, phrases and concepts used in national and local agendas and to repackage or rename services using emerging themes and terms. To do this effectively, the service and the individual library needs a clear framework which all staff understand.

Library services and individual libraries need to be able to answer the following questions (these can be posed for any project carried out, but are invaluable when setting the overall statement of the young people's service). They are similar to those set in 1985 by *Crisis or challenge*, but are more specific and targeted:

- What is the young people's service trying to achieve? What is its aim?
- What are its aims? (This will establish the values of the service.)
- What are the objectives of the service?
- What are the behaviours required to deliver this? What do we expect staff to do, how do we expect them to perform, how will they be supported?
- What tasks need to be done to meet the aims and objectives?
- What will success look like? How will we measure performance?
- What value does success add to the lives of young people?

These points can be summarized in a model, making them easier to refer to at all times. For an example of such a model, see Figure 1.6 on page 36, well regarded as a model for organizational change. If you work through all these elements it will give you an excellent basis to start from. This book discusses in depth the questions raised above, and its aim is to help you begin to develop a sound framework for children's and young people's provision in the future.

References

1   Parker, A.-M., *Crisis or challenge*, unpublished reports for SOCCEL (Society of County Children's and Education Librarians), 1985.

2   Shepherd, J., 'Crisis of confidence: the future of children's work', *International Review of Children's Literature and Librarianship*, 1 (1), 1985.

3   Library and Information Services Council, *School libraries: the foundations of the curriculum*, London, HMSO, 1984.

4   Great Britain, Statutes, The Children Act, London, HMSO, 1989.

5   Great Britain, Statutes, Education Act, London, HMSO, 1989.

6   Association for Information Management, *The review of the public library service in England and Wales*, London, Aslib, 1995.

7   KPMG/Department of National Heritage, *Contracting-out in public libraries*, London, KPMG, 1995.

8   Department of National Heritage, *Reading the future*, London, DNH, 1997.

9   Department of National Heritage, *School library services and financial delegation*, London, HMSO, 1995.

10   Department of National Heritage, *Investing in children: the future of library services for children and young people*, London, HMSO, 1996.

11   Library and Information Commission, *2020 vision*, London, LIC, 1997 (available from 2 Sheraton Street, London W1V 4BH).

12   Greenhalgh, L. and Worple, K. with Landry, C., *Libraries in a world of cultural change*, London, UCL Press, 1995.

Part 1
PLANNING FOR THE FUTURE

1

Managing change

'You were *lucky, your* children grew up in the good old days when libraries were libraries! I bet your boys used to stroll down there and spend a quiet half an hour or so choosing real *books* . . . '

'Well, things are different now', Mum snapped. 'They're back home in under ten minutes with some daft pip-pip-pipping computer game stuck under their arm, and all you hear for hours after they get back is "Shouldn't we play safe and join the RAC, Mum?". . . and "What *is* cocaine, Mum?".'

A. Fine, *Goggle-eyes*[1]

In order to ensure that the library is best placed to respond to the challenges of the future, the first step is to take an in-depth and scrupulously honest look at what is currently being offered to users, and to compare this with what ideally should be on offer. As it is often taken for granted, this stage of the process is often omitted. Development work is consequently often begun without full assessment of the situation having been made, thus resulting in many a missed opportunity.

Vested interest on the part of the senior management of a service can mean that assumptions are made as to the current position of the service and what it would like to offer. As a result, real change may not be made.

Knowing the service in detail

One way of tackling this is by setting up a small working group made up of a representative cross-section of staff to act as a design team. By working through a series of steps the group can investigate the evidence, brainstorm, take advice and produce a series of recommendations which can then be used to set the direction for the future, create the necessary sense of purpose, define the strategies and motivate the staff.

Whatever way it is decided to organize the investigation, work should progress through trigger questions such as those given below. Brainstorming is one of the best techniques of tackling these. The rules of brainstorming are that everyone within a group takes turns in stating what they think are the issues. All statements must be respected at this stage and not questioned. If someone is unable to think of anything as the facilitator goes round the circle, proceed to the next person until everyone has exhausted their ideas. Next, take the list of ideas, discuss any areas of confusion or lack of understanding, then ask the group to choose what it thinks are the key issues out of those raised. Finally, the key issues are listed preparatory to commencing more in-depth work on them.

The first stage of this work is to ask the following questions:

- what services are on offer?
- which are the best and worst aspects?
- what are the core strengths and weaknesses?
- what are the aims and objectives?
- what are the values of the service?
- what constraints are there on freedom of action?
- what is most/least likely to be popular and successful?
- what is the viability of each service?
- what new services are users likely to want in the future?
- which new services are to be introduced, and when?

What services are on offer?

The next stage of the enquiry is to list all the services that are provided to young people, remembering to include those not actually provided in the library building. This list is likely to include such items as:

- under-fives: Bookstart or books for babies, story-telling, visits to playgroups, parent toddler clubs
- children's service: homework club, activities, stock, literacy initiatives
- teenagers: teenage reading groups, stock, information
- IT: CD ROMs, Internet access
- parenting support
- information
- literacy.

Service health check

Next, either for the whole library service or for each aspect of the service you wish to review, ask yourself the following:

- Where would you place this service along a line of development or continuum stretching from 'new, exciting service' to 'at the end of its useful life'?
- Is it draining away a lot of useful resources but not earning its keep?
- Is it, while not spectacular, a foundation stone of the service?

If these questions are asked and the answers acted upon, services will remain appropriate and exciting for the users. The questions can also help in avoiding the trap of developing too many new ideas without discarding others, and of continuing an activity just because it always has been done that way.

It is now recognized that all services, like products, go through a lifecycle (Figure 1.1). A new service begins slowly and has a high cost–use ratio. As it develops it becomes a popular, low cost service. If it is not constantly reassessed and developed then it can become an expensive millstone.

For more information about this concept, the reader should investigate the Boston and Anshoff matrix.[2] This and more recent developments of the concept will enable you to chart exactly where your services are on a matrix similar to the one in Figure 1.2 below. These methods will help you to decide exactly what point a service has reached in development terms and, in cost terms, help you to decide how to allocate resources, particularly when funding is scarce.

What are the strengths of the service?

One of the most powerful ways of establishing the direction of a service and identifying what is successful and what is not, is to carry out a **SWOT analysis**. A brainstorming session will enable the identification of strengths, weaknesses, opportunities and threats and list the key issues for the service. Using the outlines below this method can be used

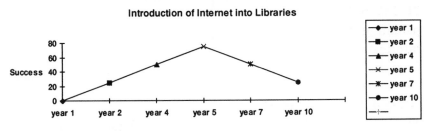

Fig. 1.1 *Product lifecycle*

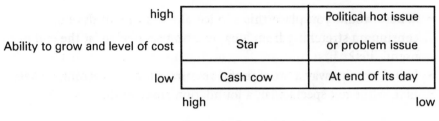

Fig. 1.2   *Matrix analysis of services provided*

either to develop a strategy for a particular section of the service or to create its overall direction. Once the initial brainstorming session has been completed the next step is to identify the six most important issues in each section which have arisen in discussion. These can then be developed into the **SWOT action plan** as issues to investigate further.

SWOT analysis

List strengths, weaknesses, opportunities and threats below:

Strengths	Weaknesses
Opportunities	**Threats**

SWOT action plan

Take the six key issues for each section from the brainstorming session and enter in the first column. Take each issue and develop an action plan to deal with it by asking what the issue means (second column) and then think of a range of ideas of how to deal with it (third column).

Key strengths	Which means that	Plan to keep it strong
Key weaknesses	**Which means that**	**Plan to overcome**
Key opportunities	**Which means that**	**Plan to develop**
Key threats	**Which means that**	**Plan to turn into strengths**

Example: SWOT analysis for services to young people 12–19 years

List strengths, weaknesses, opportunities and threats below:

Strengths	Weaknesses
Good publishing Popular Own section Own budget	Token non-fiction of the sex, drugs, rock and roll era No image or branding No information Teenagers are series driven Users are getting younger Section lost, particularly in large adult library Too many hardbacks Not attracting enough readers Falls between adult and children's buying
Opportunities	**Threats**
Work with youth and community Young people are a high political issue Get young people involved Information is around and important IT People are willing to fund services to teenagers	Youth and community information shops Other library users may object If we introduce information we will get complaints Teenagers frighten staff

Example: SWOT action plan

This is partly filled in.

Key strengths	Which means that	Plan to keep it strong
Popular	If we offer better stock we will attract more young people and issues will rise.	Market the section better. Create a recognizable branding.

Key weaknesses	Which means that	Plan to overcome
No information	Young people don't see libraries as a place for information and so we lose readers.	Develop an approach to information. Pull together all the best information from youth information shops (YIS) into fact files and then get youth and community to endorse.

Key opportunities	Which means that	Plan to develop
Involve young people	They feel they own the section, they will tell their friends and will develop it to meet their changing needs.	Set up a young people's user group and give them the teenage budget to buy stock.

Key threats	Which means that	Plan to turn into strengths
Youth information shops	May be seen to be competing, and teenagers confused as to where to go.	Work with YIS to develop an authority-wide strategy as YIS can't be everywhere. Also, sign-post young people to the shops from libraries for further information and counselling.

Making changes

SWOT analysis enables a broad overview to be taken of the service. It allows staff to stand back and identify influences and challenges, and often it has surprising results, with staff becoming very committed to the process. Having carried out a SWOT analysis to obtain an overview of provision, many issues and ideas will have been raised. It is worth adding two more linked steps. This takes the suggestions for development and allows further investigation and analysis, which can be most beneficial to the service.

STEP analysis

STEP analysis allows you to take an idea and work it against the four key issues for service development. In other words, you need to ask yourself what are the social, technological, economic and political implications of the idea. Again, a matrix is a good way to approach this and a brainstorming session will lead to the best results, as in Figure 1.3 below. You can then decide whether these issues have a positive or negative impact on service development.

Force field analysis

Having brainstormed the key strengths and opportunities, determined the aims and objectives and assessed the health of each aspect of provision and of the service as a whole, you must now address the need for change in those areas identified as requiring action.

Social	Technological
Demographic change – negative and positive	Converging technology – positive New ways of doing things – positive
Economic	Political
Funding constrained – negative New funding opportunities – positive	Tension between central and local government – negative

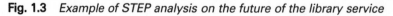

Fig. 1.3 *Example of STEP analysis on the future of the library service*

Force field analysis can help introduce change with the minimum of effort and disruption. The aim is to identify all the forces helping and hindering a situation in which change is desirable. Each force is given an arrow the length of which reflects the anticipated influence: long for major, short for minor influence. See Figure 1.4, for example.

Hindering forces press down on service provision, making it less effective and often throwing it out of balance. Helping forces meanwhile make service provision buoyant, propping it up and making it highly effective. The aim is to achieve more helping than hindering forces, or a helping force of the same strength as one that hinders, so cancelling out its impact.

Benefits of a force field analysis exercise

The benefits of such an approach to identifying the need for change are many, including:

- it often opens up new ideas for action
- it can boil a problem down to size
- it can be used by one person or by a group, and it can help to make sure that all the members of a group are on the same wavelength.

The success of the scheme depends upon the quality and completeness of the analysis, and it is important to remember that it is only the first step in managing change.

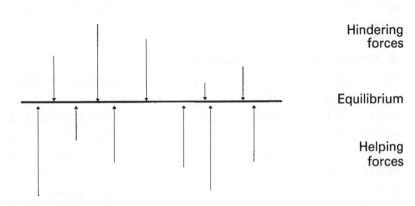

Fig. 1.4 *Force field analysis*

How to make it work

The following steps are recommended in completing a force field analysis:

- First, define the current situation clearly and determine the desired end result. In other words, assess what is happening *now* and what you would *like* to happen.
- Identify as many forces as possible – don't get bogged down with what is or isn't possible.
- Include information from as many different sources as possible.
- Check that the list of forces includes:
  - the position of influential parties
  - policies and procedures
  - the nature of individual needs and habits
  - outside forces
  - administrative practices
  - financial resources
  - stock issues.
- Consider ways of maximizing the positive helping forces and minimizing or removing the hindering forces.
- Identify forces which improve delivery and effectiveness, reduce the cost, market the service better for customers and develop the potential of employees.

Example: Improving the provision of information for teenagers

A library needs to improve information provision to teenagers. The first step is to conduct a force field analysis, as in the example in Figure 1.5 below.

A programme for change

With its opportunities and strengths identified, the core aspects of provision recognized and a method put in place for planning future developments of the less successful aspects of the service, a library or authority is ready to create a service framework. You will now have the techniques to tackle all the issues which may arise, and the framework in Figure 1.6 below offers both a service outline and a problem-solving approach to new provision, thus ensuring that developments are incremental and sustained.

If this framework is completed a high performing service should

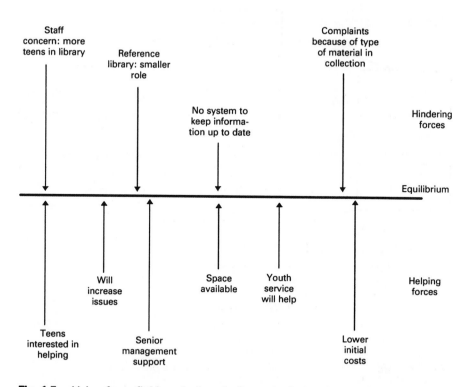

Fig. 1.5   *Using force field analysis to indicate the issues in developing teenage information provision*

result. It may well have a flattened structure with work groups taking more responsibility. Decisions will be made at the point of delivery, flexibility will be pre-eminent, information will be shared and all will be directional. Staff will be adaptable and highly employable because their work adds value. All this produces an exciting service for the users.

Change can, however, be threatening to staff and users. The environment must be right for change and it will only be successful if a combination of the elements below are in place and obvious to staff:

- a compelling need to change
- a compelling vision
- good communication of the vision
- a willingness to prescribe the future
- identified early successes
- a willingness to let go.

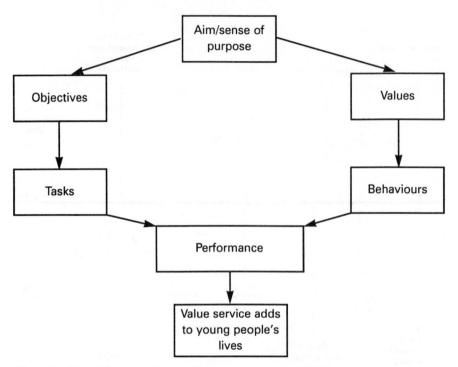

Fig. 1.6   *Model for developing all aspects of service provision*

To sustain change, feedback needs to be encouraged from staff and users, and the service needs to be assessed against others. Success and achievements must be celebrated and the past respected, not ridiculed.

In order to promote change, you need to encourage all staff to imagine how they would ideally like the service to develop. They need to be encouraged to take responsibility and to recognize that what counts, is what works. This may not necessarily be what they have been used to providing if this is no longer feasible. To find out what does work, all staff need to take responsibility, acting together to discover the choices. Preservation is not an option. Change is difficult to manage. Many people are threatened or frightened by it. They need to be helped to see that it is not what happens to them, but how they respond to what is happening, that determines the quality of their experience. How they respond is determined by the meaning they assign to an event. For example, do they feel an event is threatening, a challenge, or an opportunity? They need to be encouraged to focus on the possibilities and to anticipate the need for change.

As a manager one needs to be focused when leading a children's service or library through change, whether it takes the form of reorganizing the layout of a library, or of introducing a completely different method of provision. It is very easy to cut oneself off from future possibilities, to achieve less than one set out to do, because of one's tendency to cling to old solutions. One can put an enormous amount of energy into resisting a new solution.

If an information unit is to organize itself around its central vision and around its service objectives, then these must be both clear and consistent, as must its goals, tasks, behaviour and values. Obviously this must be true both at the senior level and at specialist and local levels. Staff need to be aware of what their goals are and how they are measured. Do they value an activity? Can they do it? Does their behaviour help or hinder others? All too often, professionals who are not children's specialists may acknowledge the need for the children's service, but will push it down to the bottom of the 'to do' list in favour of activities which they prefer, and with which they feel more comfortable.

To achieve a high-performing, effective children's service, clarity is needed at a succession of stages:

1 The providing authority's mission and strategy
2 The overall children's service strategy
3 The task list: i.e. a list of actions required to deliver the strategy
4 The task process: i.e. a 'game plan' for executing a task
5 Behaviour: i.e. the skills for 'playing the game' (*doing it*).

For a service to 'achieve', *everybody* in that service needs to share the values implicit in children's provision, and to be aware that almost every task has client care and service development implications. Above all, they need the behaviours to 'do it right'.

This belief is not only relevant to the children's library service, it is fundamental to the whole public library service. Everyone in the service should understand the purpose and values of each aspect of the service, perceive how they combine to form the overall authority vision and understand how their own job, their individual role, contributes to that vision. The children's service has no greater right to understanding than any other part of the organization and it must work at integrating into the whole service and demonstrating the ways in which it supports general provision. This will avoid alienating staff and decision-makers, and will ensure that the 'specialist versus generalist' arguments of the eighties are not reborn. We have need of both the specialist and the generalist librarian – the future is in the hands of both.

References
1 Fine, A., *Goggle-eyes*, Harmondsworth, Penguin, 1989.

2

A sense of purpose

In order to complete this project you need the resources of this library . . .
This is a *Library*.
It is *Not*
(a) a play area;
(b) a social meeting-place;
(c) a snack bar.   T. Breslin, *New school blues*[1]

The brainstorming sessions mentioned in Chapter 1 examine past provision, new opportunities and assessment of whether a project is worth
the time and cost invested in it. This allows a pause in the hectic pursuit
of day-to-day provision to think through what the service aims to
achieve. Every time this work has been carried out it has provided
renewed vigour together with an opportunity to regroup, to redefine
what the service is there for and to recommit to the future.

Every organization needs values and goals, a sense of purpose, a long-
term vision. Being clear about what these are ensures that staff know in
which direction they are going, what they are attempting to achieve,
what is important and what is worth while. Together, these issues form
the basis of a business plan. If you have worked through the techniques
in the previous chapter you will already be aware of many of the compo-
nents of the first stage of the business plan.

The benefits of business planning

Business planning ensures efficient and effective operation of activities
on a day-to-day basis, and can also help with the circumstances of an
organization change. Planning is not a one-off event: it must be done
regularly and should always precede any actions. All too often, once an
objective has been agreed, its planning is neglected. The business plan
offers a means to an end, not an end in itself.

The value of business plans is that they enable organizations to fulfil
their objectives: staff can work more effectively together because they
know what they are trying to achieve, and work can be done systemati-

cally, thus reducing conflict and confusion. Business plans must be flexible to allow for change and to cater for the occasional 'crisis', but there must be clearly laid out milestones against which progress can be checked.

Much has been written about the subject of business plans, and for many they have an impenetrable mystique. Authorities can often find that the first time they attempt to write a business plan it is an horrendous experience. Working to a corporate structure often leads to the production of a huge volume full of words and concepts. While this looks good in terms of a thick file on a shelf, the shelf is where is usually stays.

Using this structure it is relatively easy to produce a current business plan, which lays out the vision, objectives, goals and strategies for all aspects of the children's service. An annual action plan of targets for the coming year then needs to be produced. Strategies are amended and updated when required. Part 2 of this book deals with creating strategies. First, it is necessary to look at how to create a vision and a sense of purpose within an organization, using good leadership and performance measurement to achieve the desired goals.

Vision

It is vital to infuse the children's service with a sense of purpose, to release the energy and motivation of staff and to lead the service to something tangible and meaningful. A knowledge of the purpose of the service gives staff stability. When establishing a vision for your organization, think broadly and consider what business you are in, what position you want to occupy and how you can develop if you want to.

A simple statement should include the key elements of provision: literacy, the promotion and stimulation of reading, provision of information and the development of information handling skills. This statement should not be limited to the service you are currently offering, but should provide the opportunity for expansion. You are not simply in the children's book and reading business, you are part of a process which enables each child to take the first steps to a life which satisfies a full range of needs. The vision statement should capture this mood, but it need not be in minute detail: that can be covered in the objectives.

Below are some examples of vision statements:

> To motivate and help children and young people use, enjoy and value books and other resources as part of their natural development and to

encourage the use and enjoyment of the library's service to further this end. The service will aim to meet the informational, recreational, educational and cultural needs of all children and young people and encourage them to become readers and library users.

Northamptonshire Libraries and Information Service

We exist to develop enquiring minds, encourage a love of reading and stimulate the imagination of young people to ensure that libraries are for life.

Hertfordshire Libraries, Arts and Information

To encourage and foster the interest of children and young people in books and reading and provide for their leisure, education and information needs to enable them to participate fully in modern society.

Clwyd Library and Information Service

When writing your vision statement try to avoid long worthy sentences. A brief but meaningful sentence is much more memorable for staff and will remain in their minds as a constant reminder of what they are trying to achieve in their everyday work.

The vision or purpose is only the beginning. Even when you know your purpose, you still must know where you are starting from, where you want to go and how you intend to get there. It must also be a shared vision, or otherwise everyone will attempt to go about realizing it in different ways, and their efforts may even cancel each other out.

Objectives

The vision or aim statement can be expanded into a series of objectives. Objectives work to ensure that the library service is actively controlled, moving towards a destination rather than passively drifting. Objectives should challenge and motivate the staff. Ideally the whole service will have corporate objectives from which the children's service and individual libraries can derive subsidiary objectives. Even if this is not the case, children's services can develop their own objectives as long as operations in other areas are taken into consideration. Objectives are more specific than the vision statement. They must define the desired state and they must be measurable. Examples of some of the areas in which children's services might want to set up objectives are:

• The encouragement and promotion of literacy and the development of a love of reading.

- The motivation of young people to use and enjoy books and other resources as part of their natural development.
- The provision of the resources and environment to support lifelong learning and self-development.
- Assistance to enable parents and other carers to make full use of all resources available from the library.

To turn these points into real objectives it is necessary to build on work already done to identify the services offered and to focus on the key issues for the authority. The objectives should capture opportunities for the future, not just the service of today. They should allow for changes in public taste, for technical, economic and demographic factors and for political change. This is fundamental to how libraries see themselves. Libraries have changed rapidly to reflect new issues such as greater community focus, loans of audiovisual materials and compact discs, the introduction of IT and increased user need for information. We have failed to gain recognition for these developments partly because our vision and objectives are still perceived by many as being limited to the loan of fiction to the literate middle class. This *is* part of our business – but *only* part.

We can learn much from modelling vision statements and objectives on business practice. Tim Waterstone is well known in the profession for the successful children's sections in his bookshops. His next step, however, is not merely to open self-contained children's bookshops. He sees himself as being in the children's business, not just the book business, and has now opened 'Daisy and Tom' shops. These have been described as a chain of children's stores selling the widest range of merchandise and services specifically for children up to the age of ten. Included in the range will be toys, games, nursery equipment, shoes, children's hairdressing and soda bars, and he has promised that 10% of the space will be for books.

When setting objectives there are five criteria to be met. Objectives should be:

- achievable yet challenging. They will then generate energy, drive and commitment.
- clear and understandable, containing no jargon, so that they can be achieved. Consultation before agreeing the objective, and adequate briefing afterwards, are essential.

- measurable at the level where the action takes place so making it clear exactly what is wanted and by when, so that progress can be measured. If the people doing the work can do the measuring then they are often highly motivated. Not all objectives can be measured in mathematical terms, but a range of indicators can be identified which would demonstrate when an objective had been met.
- relevant and carefully researched. Objectives should make a real difference, because staff enthusiasm will otherwise soon wane.
- related to objectives or needs of other parts of the organization. This has been a fault of children's library services in the past. Their failure to take account of other areas of the service often created tension, resulting in lack of support for development.

Meeting these criteria is difficult at first. It may be worth identifying key statements of what you are trying to achieve and then applying the five criteria to each. Some examples of service objectives are listed below. They show very different approaches and support different types of service provision.

Clwyd divided their objectives into two, creating policy objectives and operational objectives:

Table 2.1   *Clwyd's approach to service objectives*

Policy objectives	Operational objectives
To encourage and support the interest of children and young people in books and reading and the use of libraries	• Ensure that all staff are appropriately trained in the provision of library services to children and young people • Arrange and coordinate an annual programme of author visits, competitions, seminars and other events to celebrate Children's Book Week • Provide year round opportunities for children to participate in book/reading/library related activities and events in libraries and other appropriate venues in the community

	• Target particular efforts at encouraging an early enthusiasm in young children for reading and books, particularly through co-operation with other agencies e.g. Playgroup Association, Health Authority, Social Services Department etc.
To provide a wide range of books and related resources to support the reading and information needs of children and young people	• Identify and select stock appropriate to the children's emotional, intellectual and aesthetic development, reading and comprehension levels and subject interest areas
	• Provide for the needs of specific client groups and target resources to groups under-using the service by designing and implementing measures to meet their needs
	• Ensure that stocks remain relevant and attractive through on-going stock-editing and stock exchanges
To provide for the development of the information skills of children and young people	• Liaise closely with schools and encourage teachers and children to take the opportunity to participate in programmes of visits to libraries and facilitate the development of information skills
	• Cooperate with the Schools Library Service in providing input to those elements of the curriculum concerned with information skills
	• To encourage and support parental involvement in children's reading
	• Contact with parents to advise them on the range of books for children and young people and the value of parent and child enjoying and sharing books and reading

- Provide and participate in appropriate events and promotional opportunities to increase parental awareness of books, reading and libraries

To provide resources, advice, training and support to statutory and voluntary services for children and young people in the community

- Liaise closely with a range of statutory and voluntary agencies providing services for children
- Provide termly collections of books to pre-school playgroups
- Deliver appropriate book related training to a wide variety of statutory and voluntary agencies delivering services to children. Participate in childcare courses being delivered through institutes of further education on a cost recovery basis.

In Leicestershire the objectives are high-level statements. They indicate that the criteria have been met (in that all are measurable), but how they are to be measured is left to further documentation. As long as the detail is thought through at the objective-setting stage, the clarity of short statements such as these often helps staff to keep the objectives in mind during their everyday activities.

The objectives for the children's and young peoples service are:

- to offer for loan and for reference books and audiovisual items, etc.
- to provide an advisory service which assists children in choosing material to meet effectively their borrowing needs
- to make available to customers, directly or indirectly, the assistance of staff skilled and experienced in the specialism
- to identify and respond to the needs of children with special requirements, including members of ethnic minority communities
- to promote the use of libraries, the love of books and reading, and the development of literacy amongst children, both directly and through support which is given to parents and carers
- to support the policies of the Education Department especially those

relating to literacy and language development and multicultural education
- to ensure cost effectiveness, particularly through:
  - developing and maintaining the total stock of the Libraries and Information Service as a single network, and with reference to both current and future needs
  - giving access to all stock from any service point via the requests and reservations service
  - monitoring the take up and quality of services to children and young people
  - developing and implementing standards/criteria for the selection, management, performance and disposal of stock, and for the management and performance of services.

Dorset's mission and objectives are:

- creating and strengthening reading habits in children from an early age
- stimulating the imagination and creativity of children and young people
- supporting the oral tradition.

Our libraries should create an environment where children will be able to explore, decide for themselves and satisfy their own needs, where they can develop their own interests which may have been stimulated by school work or which may reflect current child culture or which may have originated from other influences on the individual child.

These are just three examples of how an authority can build up its objectives from the key issues which are the business of children's libraries.

The features and benefits of the children's service

The first stage of the business plan is completed by identifying the benefits of providing the service. Identifying and knowing the difference between the features and benefits of the services being provided is a key feature of marketing. Worldwide, the library profession often complains that it does not attract enough attention from the private sector and that it is not understood. This is often because the benefits of the service are not communicated effectively.

If work is carried out in this area, and benefits are established, this can provide a great advantage upon which to base discussions with elected representatives, with users and with potential sponsors. The work described up to this point will give you much of the information required to enable you to carry out this stage of the plan.

Services are usually described as a series of features – for example, a parents' collection, or an under-fives collection. While these are useful descriptors they do not tend to excite or engage the reader. A feature describes a service. When the question 'What does that mean?' is answered, as in the SWOT analysis on page 28, the benefits of the service will be identified and the users will understand the purpose of the service because it meets a need. Users will also begin to feel that their needs are being responded to and met. A good example of this in the community is the marketing of the public swimming pool. To begin with it was invariably marketed as a swimming pool for all. When local authorities began to identify features which would benefit specific areas of the community, such as ladies' nights, toddlers' sessions and family swimming, they began to target or segment the users. The organizers then went on to identify the benefits of using the pool in this way. Ladies' nights were marketed as a time to swim safely and in peace. The up-turn in use as a result of splitting users into groups and aiming marketing specifically at each group is now legend.

Benefits need to be worked out for each customer group and the appropriate service provided. Thinking about your own purchasing decisions will help explain how people buy something because of its benefits, not just its features. An environmentalist would buy an electric car, not just because it was electric – the feature – but because it protected the environment – the benefit. This way of thinking is vital to the successful development of the children's service in times of economic restraint.

An information service for teenagers may be offered – a feature. What are the benefits? The information service means that young people:

- have easy access to relevant information
- don't have to ask for it
- find it where and when they need it
- don't have to pay for the service
- are enabled to make life choices, etc.

Once the difference between benefits and features is understood the relationship between cost and benefit can be analysed.

Reference
1   Breslin, T., *New school blues*, Edinburgh, Canongate, 1992.

3

The users of children's libraries

> Glenda, looking very learned, was sitting on the carpet in the library area,
> with books piled all round her. She was reading a comic.
>
> J. Mark, *The dead letter box*[1]

We are now in the market-led age where the focus is on the customer and
on the customer's needs. The fundamental principle to recognize is that
the library service must focus on and orientate itself around the requirements of the customer. It must supply resources or services which
groups of customers genuinely want, and it must constantly ensure that
it keeps in tune with changing needs. Marketing must be taken seriously to ensure that children's services take their rightful place in council
services and in the hearts and minds of the customers.

Grouping services and users

The children's service is one of the few sectors of librarianship which
has effectively grouped its services and users around the wants and
needs of the community it serves. It works proactively and innovatively
to exceed expectations. This has been achieved because of the rapidly
changing needs of children and of their carers as they both develop
through use of the services offered. In marketing the terms used to
describe this process are 'segmentation' and 'differentiation' of the market: in other words, the process of dividing up the total market into
niches or readily identified groups.

It is likely that work on identifying services, carrying out a health
check and discussion of the customer base will have identified the market segments that are most appropriate for the children's service. Work
on the SWOT analysis will have begun to identify the benefits and dis-
advantages to be gained by targeting these.

It is possible to create a matrix which clearly shows segmentation and
differentiation and which can then be used to identify, plan and develop
the different services for different user groups. Figure 3.1 is an example.

Age groups should be chosen which are compatible with those most

	0–5	5–7	7–10	11–13	13–15	16+	Parents and carers	Members
Special needs								
Stock								
Activities/events								
Information skills								
Layout of library								
Ethnic groups								

Fig. 3.1 *A model for segmentation and differentiation of the children's service market*

often used in the planning statistics of the local authority in question. A Census age banding may be best: in the UK the sequence is: 0–4; 5–9; 10–14; 15; 16–17.

While segmentation is valuable in ensuring that services are appropriate for the particular group in question, it is also important to continually step back and take an overview. This makes certain that provision does not become too disparate. For example, while ensuring that the service is meeting National Curriculum needs for the five- to seven-year-olds, this must also be done within the context of educational attainment for all.

The users of children's libraries

Users of the children's library service range from the newly born baby to the adult carer. Children under the age of five are a unique group in libraries, partly because they are dependent upon adults around them to take them to use the services, and partly because the children's library is the only place where they will gain access to such a wide range of free resources.

Children up to the age of 16 currently make up 20% of the population of the UK, and this is not expected to change significantly in the future. Other users are older teenagers, parents, carers, staff from Social Services and Education departments and elected representatives. Children also use the library as part of a group or club such as playgroups, Rainbows, Beavers, Scouts, Cubs, Guides, Brownies, parent–toddler groups, crèches, nurseries of all kinds and special needs groups.

Finding out what children want

Developing a service that is relevant to users is contingent upon understanding their wants and needs. One factor of this understanding is improving our ability to communicate effectively with children. Children's observations and statements must be taken seriously for the sake of their development and of our own understanding. A child's view of reality is different from that of an adult most of the time. We need to discover what their views can offer us and in what circumstances. We need to be aware of the limitations of children as sources of information but make the greatest possible use of their strengths and possibilities.

To communicate with children an open approach is needed, as is a good grounding in child development. However, every communication opportunity depends upon the individual child and adult concerned, their previous relationship, the child's previous experience in communicating (or not) and the meaning the child draws from this particular encounter with adults. There is no fixed formula for communicating with children. It requires adaptability to the characteristics of each child, each adult and each situation.

Responding to children

We know from child development texts that, as children develop their intellectual, emotional and physical needs, their states and abilities change. The range of what is possible increases and alters. Development is not, however, a steady progression from birth through to adulthood by which time the person has acquired 'adult knowledge'. Children go backwards and forwards along the developmental scale through a series of milestones.

It is important for librarians to understand these milestones in order to comprehend a child's ability to answer specific questions or to give information. We must be critical of our own conclusions about children's statements. Far too often these result in our ignoring them, misinterpreting what they say or 'talking down' to them. Think how this might look and feel to the child.

A child's ability to provide information depends upon how competent they feel, and upon their confidence in the questioner and in the setting. They are much more likely to give straight answers, rather than what they think the adult wants to hear, if they feel good about themselves, if the enquiry takes a conversational tone and if they feel they are contributing to something worth while.

Developmental milestones

It is not part of the purpose of this book to give an in-depth explanation of child development. There is a range of good texts available on this subject. Of particular relevance is Maslow's hierarchy of needs, followed by Piaget and beyond. Although quite old, a good starting point in some respects is Child's *Psychology and the teacher*.[2] To fully understand the relationship between child development and communication with children, a brief summary of the key milestones is provided below:

- 0–2: the child experiences the world in a perceptual, action-oriented, mostly non-verbal way. Information is gained from them through their actions and behaviours.
- 2–5 pre-school: The advent of language and symbolic action allows the young child to share meaning with others. At this age the child has a significant capacity for understanding and responding to adults if the subject is immediately related to the child's experiences.
- 6–12: The child begins to think about what s/he says and thinks more logically. There is a growing adult-like ability to communicate and respond; however, the motivations become more difficult to discern.

The impact of the adult questioner

Children also react to the personal characteristics of the adult. Appearance, ethnicity, gender and style will affect the child's ability to respond. The expectations, attitudes and motives of the adult will all shape the child's performance. Children give better information to some adults than others, and the more competent the adult the less competent the child needs to be.

It is clear that both the child and the adult bring objective characteristics and subjective feelings to any interaction. It is therefore important to seek information from a wide range of children and to use many different formats of enquiry. In libraries this can easily be achieved by talking to individual users, by observing children's reactions and behaviour through storytimes and activities and by targeted interviewing or surveying of children. Using a variety of methods generally leads to more valid results. The consistency of information across a number of different techniques also earns the confidence of senior managers, decision-makers or paymasters.

The Children Act

Whatever forms of communication the library plans to carry out, it must consider the safety and rights of the child. In the United Kingdom these are encapsulated in the Children Act. Any relevant legislation of the country concerned must be adhered to. If there is no legislation then the basic tenets of the Children Act are a useful guide. This does not allow a child under eight to be interviewed alone, and any plans to carry out surveys of children up to 14 must be well publicized before the event.

In the United Kingdom the National Children's Survey is recommended as a method of assessing the needs and wants of children, as it is a carefully formulated plan which differentiates between age groups. It is built on good practice and follows the international advice of the ICC/ESOMAR (European Society for Opinion and Market Research) International Code of Marketing and Social Research Practice. This stipulates that

> special care shall be taken in interviewing children. Before they are interviewed, or asked to complete a questionnaire, the permission of a parent, guardian or other person currently responsible for them (such as the responsible teacher) shall be obtained. In obtaining this permission, the interviewer shall describe the nature of the interview in sufficient detail to enable the responsible person to reach an informed decision. The responsible person shall also be specially informed if it is intended to ask the children to test any products or samples.
>
> Article 12

The guidelines also suggest that the following issues are avoided when interviewing children:

- issues which could upset or worry the child
- those which risk tension between child and parent
- those relating to a potentially sensitive family situation, for example, income, family illnesses, use of drugs or alcohol in the family
- those relating to racial, religious, and similar socially or politically sensitive issues
- those concerned with sexual activities
- those relating to illegal or otherwise socially unacceptable activities.

If there is a valid and important reason for covering any such topic then it is essential that a full explanation of this is given to the responsible person and their agreement obtained; also, steps must be taken to ensure that the child is not worried, confused or misled by the questioning.

Interviewers must be carefully selected and given special training for such work. For further information read the operating manual of the UK National Children's Survey[3] and the ESOMAR *Guidelines: interviewing children.*[4]

Children as active partners in decision-making

Traditionally the involvement of users in discussion of the service on a regular basis has been limited to adults. User groups, focus groups and surgeries are not yet common even for adults and there are very few comparable opportunities for children. The profession as a whole often seems threatened by the concept of involving people in strategic and operational issues. Realistically they cannot be involved in all developments, owing to time and complexity. Involvement is, however, extremely valuable: it gains public ownership of the development, increases public commitments and encourages alternative points of view to come forward.

Young people between the ages of five and 19 can be involved in planning, implementation and evaluation. In 1996 Leeds City Council commissioned a consultation exercise with over 2000 children aged 3–16, and the findings will form the basis of service delivery plans. The citizens' jury has made a great impact where it has been tried and this approach can work with children as well. Equally successful, despite technical difficulties, is the concept of video conferencing, where children from different parts of the country, or the world, talk to each other and to adults about their views on services.

Libraries offer a number of opportunities for involving children. Reading groups and book clubs may provide a regular source of young people who have developed the social skills to interact. These groups could be used as a basis for the development of a children's user group. Discussion here can revolve around proposed activities, stock, spending and marketing. User groups tend to be more generally focused if they meet each term to discuss developments and changes.

Project work is another approach. A new library building offers the opportunity for children to get involved in the actual building work. This can have stunning results if the property department and the building contractors are willing. A local school or schools can become involved in work on measurement and building materials and children can learn the skills of bricklaying and plastering as well as gain expertise in layout and cost of materials. Many aspects of the curriculum can be delivered in one project.

Sadly, new libraries are not common; however, involvement in smaller scale refurbishment or new service provision planning can be just as effective. Taking young people between eight and 17 book-buying can be a humbling experience. Giving them the run of a library supplier with a set amount of money can show how skilled children are and how impressive their thought for others is. Many people are concerned that this will result in giving away the bookfund. Working with a supplier where the stock is usually of a high standard means that there will not be any worrying surprises in the stock bought. Book buying with young people requires constant discussion about books and is a great opportunity to find out what are the current cult books and to share some of your favourites.

Children can also be involved in design and layout. Graphic designers can turn children's concepts into reality and getting them to work with the children can have impressive results. This can include designs for the outside of a building or for a mobile as well as for the inside. Unless you want a child-like final product it is best to take the children's artwork and use it as a basis for design. This means that a high resolution image can be produced which won't date as quickly and attracts a wider audience. It is important to explain this at the outset, and children are usually quite happy with this approach. Child-like artwork is, however, very effective in the right place, which is usually on short-term, high emotional-impact material. Obviously you need to choose the right approach for each project from the outset.

Children have the social competencies, they have knowledge of what they want. They want to be listened to. Librarians need to make that little bit extra effort to listen and to offer opportunities to involve them. The outcomes will be above and beyond expectations.

References

1   Mark, J., *The dead letter box*, Harmondsworth, Puffin, 1982.
2   Child, D., *Psychology and the teacher*, 4th edn, London, Holt, Reinhart and Winston, 1986.
3   CIPFA, *Children's plans: national survey of children's attitudes to libraries*, London, Institute of Public Finance, 1997.
4   *ESOMAR guidelines: interviewing children*, Amsterdam, ESOMAR, 1990.

4

Managing the children's service

The lady librarian gave them each an application card and told them to have it filled in by their parents.

'My Mum's out' said Victor. 'You'll be shut before I can get back again. I don't want to wait till Tuesday. Can't we take some books with us now?' 'What's the hurry?' asked the librarian. 'I know you, Victor Skelton. You've lived here for twelve years and this is the first time you've set foot in the library.'

J. Mark, *Thunder and lightnings*[1]

Library provision is only as effective as the people who provide it. Whether in a single library or in an authority-wide service, the careful management of provision is vital. A sense of purpose and strategies to achieve aims are important, but if they are not implemented by people who understand them and who are motivated then only a limited service will be available. The people side of the business requires:

- inspirational leadership
- clear values
- effective use of time
- quality training both for children's specialists and for all staff
- a high profile and helpful image which is communicated to all staff and customers
- goals which are achievable, and performance which is managed
- benchmarking
- balanced priorities
- effective communication, particularly of the value of the service
- appropriate targeting of the service to different groups
- development of relationships and partnerships
- creation and management of continual cultural change
- team working
- flexible, creative and equitable service

- maintenance of financial credibility
- value for money.

Leadership

To be successful, any organization needs inspiring leadership. Leadership is made up of a combination of personal attributes and the excellent use of tools. It is a blend, therefore, of vision, integrity, strength of character, self-belief, an ability to focus on outcomes, coaching, commitment, teamwork, understanding and 'walking the job'. The 'right' attitudes are the foundation of being able to lead well and consistently at all levels.

Vision

Good leaders are able to turn ambition into reality, articulating a vision which 'hooks people in' by understanding what motivates them. It gives people direction and a firm foundation for the future. In this way a leader is able to develop a shared sense of purpose and commitment in staff, thus turning the vision developed on the page into something meaningful for every member of staff. If this understanding does not exist, the vision will not be turned into action and the service will be ineffective. The leader must also continually fine tune the vision, setting the stage for new ambitions in order to ensure that the service continually moves forward. Vision is not just doing things right – it is doing the right things.

Integrity

Personal and professional integrity is vital in leadership. Without it there will be neither trust nor honesty within a service, and, without this, people will cease to think and innovate. Successful leaders make time for themselves and for others, continually involving staff in development of the service. They show that people matter and they understand the characteristics which inhibit progress in themselves and in others and work to overcome them.

Strength of character

An effective leader is able to take risks and to turn dreams into reality. This requires courage and free thinking, and it is the quality of the courage that is important. It is important to get the balance right between bureaucracy and development: to take risks but within limits, thus ensuring that the whole service is not sabotaged in the process.

Self-belief

Ability and determination are the key elements of self-belief. There is a need for confidence but not arrogance; for acceptance that things will go wrong but continual striving to make situations work; and for celebration of achievements. People who believe in themselves are willing to continue to learn and to help others grow.

Focus on the outcomes

It is the responsibility of leaders to determine the hopes and aspirations for the coming year, and it is necessary for them to act with decision and clarity. By focusing on results, a leader can motivate staff into action because they will begin to understand the impact of their work on the success of the service, and will begin to understand why goals and objectives have to be clearly defined and measurable. This focus also ensures that an organization will develop, and that it will concentrate on quality.

Coaching

A leader needs great strength and humility in order to get the best out of people. S/he needs to build on individual abilities, creating a positive profile for each member of staff and quietly strengthen weaknesses and reinforce strengths. This necessitates being in touch with staff and putting people first, giving them responsibility so that they can act decisively.

Commitment

It is easy for a leader to think that s/he has reached the top and to relax, when in fact the hard work has only just begun. Commitment means getting others to work with and for you; setting high, realistic goals, believing in the future of the service, seeing the competitive edge, understanding finance, having a high-level drive, being self-confident and accepting fluidity.

Team work

Teams have to be built and maintained. The effective leader needs to know how to do this. Teams must perform and learn together over a period of time in order to achieve results, each member of the team knowing what to do and being aware of the ways in which their ideas add value. The ideal number for a team is between six and seven, and each team needs a coordinator, an 'ideas' person, a monitor, a 'builder' and a 'doer'. There has been a fair amount of work done on team roles, and there are a number of techniques to establish the preferences of individuals. Belbin[2] and Myers-Briggs[3] are probably the best known and easiest to understand.

Understanding and attention

A leader needs total commitment to the service to get the best out of everyone, and there is little time to be concerned about their own rank and status. They need to listen and provide time to staff to enable them to give of their best, and they need to be approachable at all times.

'Walking the job'

To achieve all this a leader must lead by example. An effective leader will understand what makes people want to work for the service, will treat all equally and will create a positive atmosphere and tone for an organization. S/he must be seen, must listen, must be aware of the impact s/he makes. A leader must manage by example, must make time for others and must be sincere, fair and responsive. Leaders must also reserve their planning and working for inside their own office so that they are free to listen and observe the service in action. They must also be willing to change if they find they are delivering the wrong message.

In order to be a good leader, it is necessary to be a team player and to avoid adversarial thinking; to create time to reflect in order to achieve self-learning, creativity and motivation. The following tips sum up what a good leader needs to succeed in developing a service, with full staff support and with minimum disruption and distress to all concerned. They are particularly useful pointers in times of change:

- develop trust and rapport
- help people to let go of outdated ideas
- continually specify, clarify and define desired outcomes
- commit to the desired outcome
- focus on what is happening now: this helps to avoid being obsessed by the past and fearing the future

- remain flexible and able to respond to new situations
- focus on what works for your organization
- remove the 'blame' culture
- acknowledge negative emotions but ask what needs to happen now
- suspend judgment
- if resistance arises, explore it and use it rather than reacting to it and creating a battle of wills
- focus on going beyond winning
- give permission to everyone to win
- analyse what you are doing unsuccessfully
- search for alternative ways of expressing the recommended change that will satisfy the situation
- ask 'what if . . . ?'
- use humour to manage
- be willing to identify new opportunities and go beyond the traditional habits of the organization
- seek out the unexpected
- make time for everyone
- accept the stress needed to motivate you to a higher level of planning.

Values

Many organizations publish a clear set of statements which define what their values are. This is quite a difficult section to write at the beginning of a business plan, yet it is one of the most powerful and valuable. A defined set of values can create harmony within an organization by identifying the culture of the service, by determining how decisions are made, how work is done and how others are treated. Values allow everyone to know where they are in an organization, how they fit in and what their objectives are. Alternatively, values are often implied through the vision, strategy and objectives of the plan. The same conclusions can be drawn from this approach but, because they have to be searched for within the plan they can often be missed, and confusion can arise. It is worth taking the time to be explicit about what your organization values. The values of an organization usually include statements covering:

- **People**
  There is nothing more important to a service than its users and its staff. It is the interplay between the two which makes the difference

in how successful an organization can be. Achievement of its vision depends upon personal accountability and of individual effort to continuously add value. Value statements in relation to people usually cover support, commitment and involvement, the working environment, rewards and recognition, the role of teamwork, personal accountability and development and training opportunities.

Issues often covered include: the development of a learning organization; staff as pioneers, not passengers; collaboration, cooperation and partnership; people-friendly organizations; equal opportunity for all and celebration of diversity.

- **User needs or customer service**
  How the service perceives its users defines the way in which they are treated. Customer care is a fundamental value and still requires an overt statement of intent. It is so easy to assume that we know what the user wants and needs that we get immersed in day-to-day provision and forget that we are dealing with individual people. Statements usually express the hope that we should anticipate needs and strive to meet or exceed all reasonable expectations. Services to users should be what they want – reliable, appropriate, centred on the user, equally available to all, neutral and unbiased. Libraries have much on which to pride themselves in relation to readers. Research shows that readers feel safe in libraries, but is the same level of support offered to all? Are children treated as equal to adults?

- **Financial discipline**
  Clear financial responsibility and accountability is crucial, and financial probity must be understood. Most authorities prepare a general financial statement of who can do what and what is expected of staff. The children's service often has a delegated budget and may use different book suppliers from those used by adult services, sometimes even tendering separately. The expectations of the organization concerned must be clear so that staff know the parameters within which they can operate. For example, who is entitled to negotiate deals with suppliers? What negotiations can take place at suppliers' showrooms? What discounts can be agreed by whom?

- **Consistent and ever-increasing quality**
  The customer service statement specifies how users should be treated

but we also must be clear about the level of service they can expect. Staff need to know what level of service to provide. The best library services are continually searching for a consistent and ever-increasing quality of provision, with staff ceaselessly engaged in assessing effectiveness and searching for improvement. If a library service is committed to quality, it must have an infrastructure to measure the degree of quality achieved. This should include management statistics, user surveys, audits and unobtrusive testing. All this requires the achievement of excellence through focused activity and ruthlessness in shedding activity no longer valued by the user.

- **Safe environment**
  The value placed by an organization on its working environment says a lot about the organization concerned. Safety is particularly important for children, and value statements should cover both staff working conditions and provision for users. The security of children needs to be high on the agenda as they are very vulnerable in today's society. With the additional problem of reduction of staffing in children's areas, sight lines must be carefully constructed, and good use must be made of video cameras and mirrors. Furniture must be made safe, panic buttons must be available in all rooms and safety doors must be in place. The importance of this cannot be overestimated and the library service should have a clear understanding of potential problem areas and a commitment to improvement within these. Relevant issues, including ideas for implementation, are discussed in more detail in *Children and young people: Library Association guidelines for public library services*.[4]

- **Diversity and culture**
  We live in a multicultural society made up of individuals with many needs, beliefs and principles. This should be reflected in the values of the organization. A clear understanding of the diversity of information and experience available to the service should be provided. This should relate not just to users but to all the staff as well.

- **Innovation, timely decision-making and organizational flexibility**
  It is crucial to adapt quickly as priorities change, and the ability to produce new ideas and turn them into action is essential. New services need to be developed as well as existing ones improved. Staff

should feel that they have a key role in service development, and there should be a communication structure which allows their ideas to be heard. Lessons will be learnt from new working patterns.

- **A sense of community**
  A public library service is there to serve its community, but how it defines that community, who is included within it, what importance is allocated to it and how the library service communicates with it, all set the tone of how the service is to be provided. Services with a clear sense of the importance of the library and its role in the locality will be a customer-driven organization committed to improving opportunities. Knowing what is important to the community brings synchronicity, depth and endurance.

- **Integrity and trust**
  The integrity and trust of an organization are often what a service is measured by. In the political environment of public libraries this is even more important. Service and personal integrity should be unequivocal in order to gain the confidence of users and paymasters. How integrity is measured should be clear. The delegation of decision-making and the valuing of all staff are key aspects, as is the day-to-day performance of the service. Integrity and trust are determined from the top, and the actions of senior management are often used as a yardstick to judge the whole service.

- **Personal values**
  These have to be balanced with service needs. Conflict can emerge because an individual is unable to perceive the bigger picture of the whole library service and their role within it. Alternatively, conflict may occur when personal values are compromised because of a decision made by the service. This may become even more of an issue as services take on sponsorship and partnership working. Staff need to be clear that when their personal values are recognized, it is the service values which take precedence.

All these are delicate, often sensitive issues as they can run contrary to individuals' personal principles and life objectives. Their importance is usually underestimated or ignored, or it is simply hoped that they will be adopted by staff by a kind of osmosis. The importance of clear, explicit value statements are equally relevant for the library service as a whole, for the children's service, for an individual library or for the children's section within that. These statements should, of course, build upon each other and inter-relate. Confusion, inappropriate behaviour and poor service can all be avoided if people know what is expected of them, what type of organization they are working for and what they can expect in return.

Managing the time available

To achieve all of the above, whether in the role of the children's specialist in a single library or as the head of a large children's service, the management of time is crucial. The old adage 'time is money' is misleading in library terms. It is better to see time as a resource and money as the measure of how much value you can create. Time should be viewed as an opportunity rather than a restraint. There are many in-depth studies of this subject,[5–7] but, as a brief introduction, the key issues to be considered are:

- **Focus** your mind and attention to maximize the use of time. Focus the minds of those you manage in order to ensure that they continue to move in the strategic direction taken by the service. Ask: 'Is it relevant? What is the main objective? Are we moving towards our objectives?'

- **Delegate:** add value in areas in which you can really make a difference. Delegating to others, when done properly, can enthuse and empower.

- **Action:** assign action to pertinent suggestions, don't just sit and talk about them. Ensure that all important points are identified and that everyone agrees a course of action. So much time can be wasted in unravelling misunderstandings later.

- **If it is not important, let it go:** define very specifically what is important to your job and to your service, then be ruthless about dispensing with everything else.

- **Assemble the information, make the decision and move forward:** unless it is critical to do so, don't waste time agonizing over the decision. It is important to focus on something and start moving.

- **Keep things simple:** pare things down to the bare minimum, particularly written communications.

- **People are important:** you accomplish things through people, so give them your time. If you listen to them, they will not only give you ideas but also feedback.

- **Respect other people's time:** make meetings productive, go into them with objectives, adhere to the agenda, ensure that everyone leaves with agreed actions and dates for completion of tasks.

- **Personality:** this matters to people. Balance intense focus with calmness and interest in people's ideas. In other words, don't be so committed to time management that people can't tell who you are. Focus on the issue at hand, but be you.

- **Know when to quit:** martyrdom wastes time!

Managing staff performance

Better people management is the single most important concept to make an impact on business development. You need to get superior performance from your staff and you need to do this by focusing on them. Good performance management promotes self-responsibility and motivation to perform at peak, and counselling and coaching will encourage staff to continue along these lines. Individuals need to understand the necessary tasks in order to achieve strategy, and the different skills that are needed in different situations. Staff must be managed as a whole and as individuals. The goals of the service must be clear and the individual's role in delivering the goals must be understood. Staff appraisal must be set against objective service goals and must concentrate on the competencies required to deliver those goals. The potential of junior staff needs to be tapped to a far greater degree. Their role is too often neither made clear nor encouraged. At times their initiative is even quashed. The phrase 'customer care' is taken to mean 'being nice plus getting the answer right', and many people think that 'getting the answer right' is really the only important part. Very few people go on to think of proactivity, innovation, and exceeding expectation.

Styles of management

There are, of course, a range of different styles of management. Each individual has a predominant style but may use others in certain situations. A clear understanding of one's style of management is very valuable, and, once understood, it can be modified if it doesn't fit in with the style of the organization.

The continuum in Figure 4.1 shows the different styles of performance management, progressing from the directive style on the left to the helping style on the right. Figure 4.2 gives a breakdown of the styles.

There are four stages in staff management. To begin with, the manager directs, setting the boundaries and rules. As confidence rises, early motivation often decreases, and now the manager begins to coach, helping staff to fit into the system. Staff soon begin to perceive the direction in which the service is going; they have ambition, but motivation goes up and down. Gradually the manager gives up the directive style instead providing support to staff and prompting their ideas. By taking the role of a good listener, someone to try out ideas on, s/he gradually counsels staff into greater and professional development.

Learning from others

Many different sections of the children's service have for many years shared information and good practice. This has been instrumental in its ability to take a leading role in the resurgence of librarianship now taking place. To develop new services and to assess how current provision matches that in the wider world, the willingness to learn from others and to understand and adapt examples of outstanding practice is crucial.

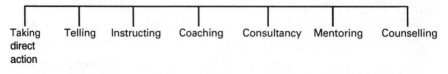

Taking direct action   Telling   Instructing   Coaching   Consultancy   Mentoring   Counselling

Fig. 4.1   *Continuum of management styles*

Directive

The directive manager is unlikely to be using counselling skills. The behaviour is:

- problem centred: offering practical solutions and doing something to sort problems out.
- manager centred: the manager is thinking about her/himself and limits her/his help to what s/he knows and feels at the time.
- directive: the manager takes charge, assumes an understanding of the situation and make decisions.
- expert: the manager brings about any changes, taking the role of controller and expert.

These styles are used if:

- the individual needs to learn a skill quickly
- there is only one person with the authority to take action
- there is a crisis
- the strategy or procedure determines what you have to do.

Dominant style

If this style is used consistently

- the organization is unable to move quickly enough
- staff say 'yes but' to new ideas
- the service provides what it thinks fit
- the focus is on problems
- staff mentally retire
- people feel disempowered
- development is always approached one way

In other words, you are a 'dinosaur'.

Helping

Counselling skills will be used to varying degrees. The further to the right of the continuum, the more the manager is being:

- person centred: helping another person to solve the problem, focusing on how they think and feel, what the issues are and what the person wants to do.
- the enabler: encouraging another person to bring about change, thus placing the manager in the role of enabler and facilitator of learning.
- non-directive: making responses that help people to think through problems and issues, identify possible solutions, decide what to do and then act independently.

These styles are used if:

- the aim is to encourage staff to take responsibility for an area of work
- there is no predetermined solution
- the approach is according to personal preference and choice
- the aim is to increase commitment to change.

Dominant style

If this style is used consistently staff are encouraged to

- develop new ideas and be customer-oriented
- focus on opportunities
- be highly motivated
- develop a high level of innovation and initiative
- welcome new approaches

In other words, you are a 'dolphin'.

Fig. 4.2 *Management styles*

A great deal can be learnt both from within a service and from colleagues further afield, both at home and abroad. It is equally valuable to look beyond the profession and examine what other businesses and organizations are doing. This could take the form of looking around the high street to see how others market to the same users and trying out their approach to customer care, or investigating the management approaches of companies in totally different areas.

Why learn from others?

Learning from others involves comparing practices and procedures and identifying ways in which the children's service can make improvements. In business this is called benchmarking. New standards and goals can then be set. This helps a service to focus on the external environment and can improve efficiency and effectiveness. It promotes a climate of change, and this change is within the hands of the staff, who are closely involved in the process. It enables them to assess what they are currently achieving and what is being achieved by others, thus becoming aware of the possibilities. By involving the staff in this way, they come to 'own' the process and thus become ambassadors for change.

The benefits of benchmarking

Benchmarking helps to set goals. It accelerates and manages change, improves processes and systems, encourages staff to see outside their day-to-day world – 'to think outside the box' – and it generates an understanding of high quality performance. It is a useful vehicle for learning, and it encourages involvement and creativity. It is also a powerful agent in the empowerment process, as it encourages individuals to take greater responsibility.

How to benchmark

There are six steps to follow in any benchmarking exercise:

1 Identify and understand current systems and processes – otherwise the comparison may be based upon the wrong issues or data.
2 Agree which organizations to benchmark against.
3 Collect information either by visiting or telephoning companies or by reading published literature.
4 Identify the best practices from the information gathered, and then consider the differences between this and your own current systems and processes.

5 Brainstorm ideas on how improvements or developments could be made and plan how to implement these changes.
6 Incorporate a review stage in order to set and evaluate targets.

Pitfalls

The benchmarking process is a great motivator but it must relate directly to service priorities. If it lacks leadership, perseverance, planning and focus, there will be problems. It requires management support and full staff participation. Lastly, it must relate to the wants and needs of users and must stay within its time frame.

Key success factors

Benchmarking will be successful if:

- the focus is on the right partners
- the service is willing to change
- the provision being benchmarked links to a sense of purpose or mission
- the focus is on the right issues
- the objectives are identified and measurable targets are set
- the senior management of the service is committed both to the process and to the outcomes
- the people involved have been given enough influence throughout the service to effect change.

The achievement of change and service development is not easy, and it requires careful management. Benchmarking – sharing good practice and learning from others – is an extremely useful part of this process. It will, however, only prove as useful as the improvements that result from it. One of the most difficult aspects to manage is that of encouraging staff to benchmark with organizations in the private sector or in businesses in totally different areas. Obviously only those from which something can be learned should be used, but it is still very difficult to get beyond reactions such as 'it couldn't happen here' or 'it's all right for them, they are in the private sector'. Time must be allowed to ask 'Why?' or 'Why not?' and to work through the reasoning involved, thus unwrapping layers of prejudice or misunderstanding. With time and a little perseverance the rewards can be stunning.

References

1   Mark, J., *Thunder and lightnings*, Harmondsworth, Puffin, 1976.
2   Belbin, M., *Team roles at work*, Oxford, Butterworth Heinemann, 1993.
3   Bayne, R., *The Myers-Briggs type indicator: a critical review and practical guide*, London, Chapman & Hall, 1995.
4   *Children and young people: Library Association guidelines for public library services*, 2nd edn, London, Library Association Publishing, 1997.
5   Godefroy, C. H. and Clark, J., *The complete time management system*, London, Piatkus, 1990.
6   Garratt, S., *Manage your time*, London, Fontana, 1985.
7   Stephen, R. and Merrill, A. R., *First things first*, Simon and Schuster, 1994.

5

Managing performance

you will put the books back on the shelves Jackus. Carefully and in order, checking the numbers on the spine

G. Cross, *The dark behind the curtain*[1]

'Aircraft are under Transport' said the librarian pointing over her shoulder with a pen.

J. Mark, *Thunder and lightnings*[2]

Libraries should develop an increasing hunger for measured improvement in all aspects of service provision. Whether managing the children's service in a single library or within a whole authority, it is vital to know how well it is performing. The service strategies described in Part 2, can be used as a specification for service delivery, or they can be summarized in a few key points. The role of the specification is to detail what each library will deliver. It sets standards for the basic level of service and determines targets for future development.

Authority-wide specifications can only be general in nature. Each library needs to examine the standards and assess how near local provision is to meeting them. Local circumstances need to be taken into consideration and the standards modified to reflect this. This does not imply a lessening of the effectiveness of the standards. Some libraries lag so far behind the standards that they need to set a two or three year programme in order to move towards achieving it. Other standards may be impossible to meet and a modified standard may be agreed. For example, a library in a community which is mostly elderly will have significant difficulty reaching a target child borrower figure of 20%.

The benefits

The benefits of measuring service delivery will mean that a service will know how well each library is performing. This in turn means that:

- improvement work can be directed towards the libraries which need support

- prompt action can be taken to sort out stock problems
- lessons can be learnt from libraries above their target level
- local staff will take greater responsibility for the service
- borrower profiles enable services to be targeted
- budget can be clearly related to need
- a downward spiral can be avoided.

The pitfalls of quantitative measures

Performance management often relies upon quantitative measures. The collection of statistics in particular can become addictive and there are some pitfalls to avoid:

- Don't use only statistics to paint a picture of service delivery. They should be used to ask questions such as: What does this tell me? Why is this so far away from the norm? etc.
- Ensure that everyone has a common understanding of why the information is being collected and how to interpret it.
- Don't collect information just for its own sake. Make sure that you use it and that staff see it being used.
- Before collecting information on a particular aspect of the service, think long and hard about the long-term impact of the collection of the data on service provision. For example, if a standard is set for the total stock figure for each library, the result is often an extensive but dog-eared and under-used stock because, in a rush to meet or beat the standard, the priority for staff becomes quantity, not quality.
- When data are linked to a formula, make sure that the potential long-term impact is thought through. For example, if the amount of stock held is linked to the staffing formula, hoarding of stock is a potential outcome.
- Don't use only one set of data even if it *is* linked. A complex matrix of a number of interrelated factors avoids abuse. For example, if the only formula worked out is the ratio of staff cost to issues, it is open to easy abuse, particularly in automated libraries.
- Don't set any standards at all unless they really are intended for use and it is proposed to use the results to manage the service.
- Ensure that quantitative measures form less than 40% of your whole quality management scheme.

Performance management in the children's library

The first step in instigating a performance measurement scheme is to find out what the whole service is doing in terms of specification and standard setting. Where possible, the children's service should be integrated within a whole service approach. If this is not yet the case then work can begin separately in the children's section, but whenever an opportunity arises to cooperate with the whole service it should be taken.

There are a number of very useful indicators to help in managing the children's service. They break down into three basic sections:

- the children and their carers
- stock
- the budget.

The Library Association children's guidelines[3] outline how to create standards and targets for a children's service. It is hoped that eventually there will be more sets of figures to compare and finally a common set of targets agreed.

Setting the standard

Relating standards to size of community

The first step in setting the standard is to decide whether standards will be common across the board or whether they will be ranged along a scale in relation to size of library or community services. Many authorities band or group together those libraries which serve similar sized communities. This is quite important when considering children's libraries because levels of use in different sizes of communities are totally different. Level of use in children's libraries is also different from adult use. For example, libraries serving large communities show a smaller proportional use by children than the average for those in small communities. If banding or grouping is not used, standards can still be set, but there must be awareness of the differing trends when analysing the results.

Community profile

At whatever point you are starting, you need a clear understanding of the community you are serving. You need to profile your community, defining the boundaries, then find out the number of people in each age band, what community groups exist, the number of institutions and groups there are in the area, what languages are spoken, how much deprivation there is and what amenities exist in order to help you learn more about the wants and needs of your community. Having created a community profile, you will be able to summarize the type of service which different groups or ages of user are entitled to, which services are free, which are charged for and what facilities are available. Having established who you are serving and what they are entitled to, you will then be able to set standards and assess performance statistically for the service you provide.

Stock management

The most straightforward aspect to measure is stock, and this is well worth undertaking as you will gain valuable information either to aid provision in a single library, or authority-wide. Library automation management data provide most of the information but, if not available, a one in ten count is well worth the effort. The most useful figures to measure are:

- the percentage of children's stock allotted to each section, which shows whether your library is in balance with your community
- the average number of issues for each section, which provides you with the relative turnover of each section and helps you see which areas are being heavily borrowed. Where there is a low turnover, is this because the stock is in use in the library or is the stock no longer relevant?
- age of stock. Different types of stock have different lifespans, and this should be fully understood. Wide variations from the target may uncover an unedited stock, lack of targeted spending or, very occasionally, very careful borrowers who look after what they read!

Two other measures, quality of stock and coverage, have to be worked out manually and are subjective and qualitative. You might use a list of authors to provide some sort of objective measure. Alternatively this can provide a very valuable peer group exercise, with librarians assessing each other's stock. These are valuable measures because they gauge quality as well as quantity. They can also provide more analytical detail to an assessment. For example, if a library achieves a long lifespan for picture books of high quality, this indicates careful use and efficient management of stock. The same assessment would not be made for non-fiction, where lifespan is an even more important factor in assessing the relevance of an item.

Other measures can be added to inform a piece of work you want to follow up. For example, if you wished to assess and improve (where necessary) special needs provision or multicultural provision, you could add a qualitative measure of coverage in each stock area. As qualitative measures take time, staff must be informed that these are part of an ongoing development plan which needs to be taken seriously.

Collecting statistics of library use can also be valuable, and this can involve counting enquiries, events and visits. Figure 5.1 gives an example of a proforma that can be used to collect data.

Community Profile

Community	Numbers	Numbers of borrowers Target	Registered Actual	% of the population registered	Active Target	Borrowers Actual	% of the population
Children as a % of population							
Numbers 0–4							
5–8							
9–11							
12–15							
16–19							
Total							
Numbers of groups: Childminders							
Playgrous							
Parent/toddler groups							
Schools including nurseries							
Special needs groups							
Family centres							
Opportunity groups							
Cultural groups (use CRE*)							
Activity clubs							
Youth clubs							
Before/after school clubs							

% borrowers who are children	Target	Actual	Languages spoken
Formal consultation opportunities			

Fig. 5.1 Proforma for setting the standards

*Council for Racial Equality

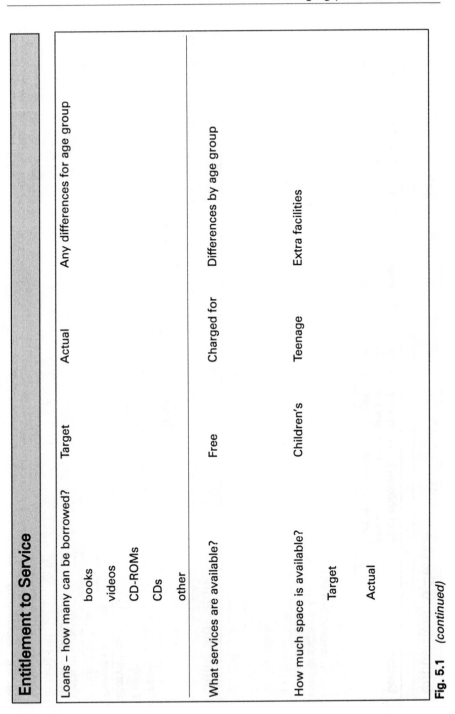

Entitlement to Service

Loans – how many can be borrowed?	Target	Actual	Any differences for age group
books			
videos			
CD-ROMs			
CDs			
other			
What services are available?	Free	Charged for	Differences by age group
How much space is available?	Children's	Teenage	Extra facilities
Target			
Actual			

Fig. 5.1 *(continued)*

Entitlement to Service

Section	% of children's stock		Average issues per annual item		Coverage	Condition	% of total children's budget	
	Target	Actual	Target	Actual	Actual	Actual	Target	Actual
Picture books								
Fiction (breakdown into smaller sections if figures available								
Non-fiction								
Talking books								
Videos								
Teenage								

Other Indicators

	Target	Actual
Enquiries		
Events		
Storytimes		
Teenage activities		
Reading groups		
Visits to schools		
Training attended		
Training run		
Talks		

Fig. 5.1 (continued)

What to do with the results

Informing the users and decision-makers
Information collected in this way can be used very effectively. If there is no access to a statistician within your service, a simple spreadsheet on a PC can give you very professional results. The leading programs come complete with step-by-step guides on screen, so you can easily calculate percentages and turn your columns of figures into impressive charts.

Pie charts are an effective way of showing the public the way the book-fund is spent or the turnover of stock in each category, i.e. the number of times on average a library issues a book during the year. Figure 5.2 gives examples:

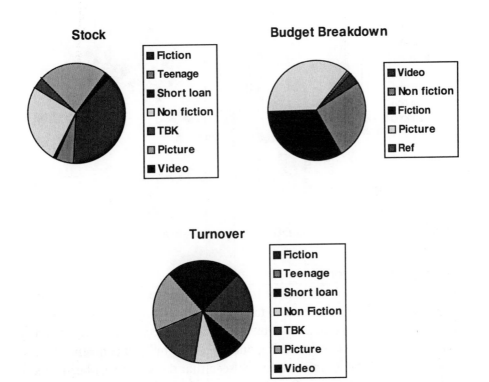

Fig. 5.2 *Examples of pie charts*

Showing children's use and stock as a proportion of the whole library, or of the whole service, can also prove very useful in arguing budget share. The chart in Figure 5.3 compares a breakdown of borrowers and a breakdown of use:

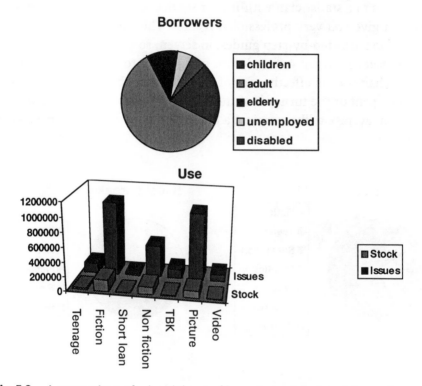

Fig. 5.3   *A comparison of a breakdown of borrowers and a breakdown of use*

Service development
The figures collected can also be valuable in offering an overview of the library service. It is fairly easy to tackle a single aspect of provision and to set targets based upon that, but you can be more effective by looking at all your figures together and working out what they tell you collectively.

In Figure 5.4, for example, it can be seen that the service has been effective in tackling the age profile of stock, but the lack of relatively straight lines elsewhere on the graph shows that other aspects now need to be grasped. If you use this scatter graph approach the issues will become clear. The system will probably be able to show an average line or even deviation away from the average. While this is useful, it can lead to obsession with graphs and distract from searching for the actual causes of a

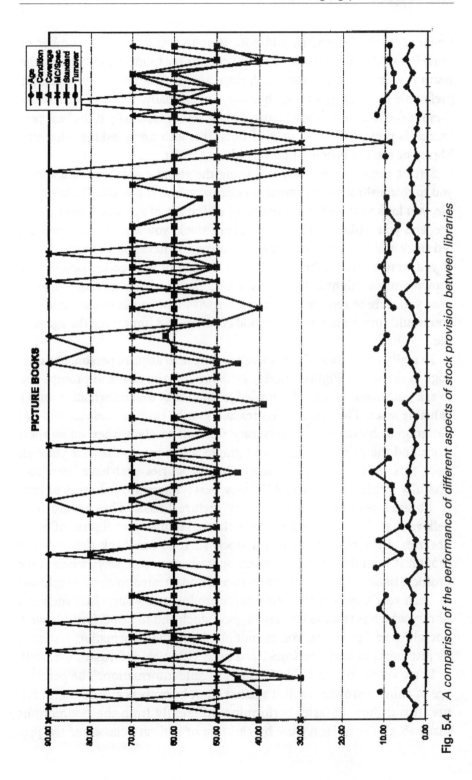

Fig. 5.4 *A comparison of the performance of different aspects of stock provision between libraries*

problem in the library. In addition, if your graph covers a number of libraries which all do stock work in order to try to meet the average, the result is a change in average which may cause frustration to set in. It is far preferable to set targets for each library individually. You may wish to set these at the level of the best results or just below, especially if the best performer is performing well on all fronts. It is also worth asking what this library or section is doing that the others are not.

Setting targets in this way and using the visual graph approach allows you to think through the impact of change across the board. If, for example, you looked at a library which had a high age of stock but good coverage, and you wished to reduce the age of stock, you would then weed the old stock and replace it with new (assuming you have the money to do so). If you were to simply buy new books from approvals collections or at a showroom you might immediately impact negatively on coverage. If, however, you were to replace worn out titles with new copies of the same title you would then be maintaining good coverage and improving the age profile.

To really make these figures work you have to acquire personal knowledge of the stock. Figures merely give you information and prompt you to ask questions: it is local knowledge that turns this information into a valuable asset. The value of figures and graphs such as these should not be ignored, however. It is very easy for staff to claim they know their stock and their users. Figures and graphs allow you to distance yourself from this subjectivity and uncover horror stories that have been successfully hidden by claims of 'I know best'. There are examples of staff in libraries possessing woefully few picture books. They would only believe that they had too few when shown comparative figures of other libraries. Libraries which hoard stock such as hardback fiction, even though it is under-used, will often only change their ways when stock profiles, issue figures and turnover are demonstrated to them graphically. Each year's work with these figures produces new surprises, such as a library which is assumed to have a good stock and to be performing well, but which in fact is not. You cannot obtain all the information you need by just working with the stock: you need statistical information as well.

Borrower profiles provide further valuable information. The percentage of child borrowers ranged against adult borrowers gives a useful figure. It can show libraries performing differently from the assumptions made about them. Heavy use by children of a library classed as the preserve of the elderly, and consequently stocked that way, is just one example. Borrower profiles can thus ensure that the budget profile is adapted to suit the actual user range. With all this information clearly presented you can plan your stock and budget allocation, target your activities and plan your service strategy. This approach allows you to take an holistic approach to children's provision.

Measuring quality

Measuring things makes it easier to manage them. But what should we be measuring? How should you measure the productivity of a children's specialist, or of any other member of staff? How should you measure the impact of an activity, or the quality of your stock? How should you assess whether what you are offering adds value to the service? Of course you should not simply count the 'through-put' described above. It is a nonsense merely to talk about issues, turnover or age of stock by themselves. These things certainly matter but they hardly make up the whole picture. Moreover, they are not the key indicators of good performance. Generally, they have been chosen because they are seen as 'objective' and therefore 'good'.

If the question is turned around we must then ask ourselves, 'Can a good children's service be distinguished from a bad one?' The answer must be, 'Yes, it can', and this is not merely measured in terms of the number of picture books issued in a day. Instinctively, subjectively, we know what are the core competencies for success. Good children's libraries seem to care a lot. Young people, parents and carers like them. What they do seems to work, reading levels go up and users come back. How do you measure that?

Soft qualitative measures recognize the inherent subjectivity of children's librarianship. These subjective driving forces – perceptions, prejudices, feelings – are the stuff of librarianship. Most successes are not rationally or logically based, they are psychologically based, and the sooner we recognize this in our assessments, the better. People can change. We should be looking at such irregular tests as how staff are improving, whether they are liked, whether customers enjoy their company or their service and whether users are achieving the success they want. In the UK the National Children's Survey helps here by asking questions such as these.

The key to using qualitative indicators is to measure improvement or value added to the service, so it is essential that you know your starting point. Before you introduce a new service, or change a layout or approach, you will need to measure people's understanding of it, together with its level of use. Then, after you introduce your change to the service, you will need to measure the same aspects again.

Quality monitoring

User groups, focus groups and customer comments systems which give user feedback all help to achieve quality monitoring. It is also important to have a formal quality monitoring programme. This is an annual check on the provision of service available to a user. It is ideal if the children's service fits into an overall policy, but if this is not possible a separate children's programme should be developed.

Quality monitoring is designed to assess systems and processes rather than the individuals who operate them. It usually combines a number of different approaches:

- unobtrusive enquiry testing, where each library is tested against a series of enquiries made in person by individuals unknown to the staff
- telephone testing, where the response to a query is assessed
- service monitoring, where the library is assessed against a checklist covering presentation, stock, administrative routines, corporate image, health and safety, and staff.

All of these checks are carried out by observation, without warning and by 'mystery' members of the public, i.e. those unknown to staff. There should be a clear checklist of the standards expected and these should be taken from the service specification. The results of the monitoring are scored, and each library will be given access to its score so that it will be able to use the results in its future target setting. While such an approach often causes concern at its introduction, there is always the possibility of staff carrying out their own monitoring. Often after the monitoring process has been carried out two or three times it becomes an acceptable and often positively anticipated part of performance management.

Quality monitoring and the children's service

Quality monitoring within the children's service can be extremely valuable as there is often concern that not all library staff like children or feel that the children's library is important. It is also another way of involving young people in the development of the service, as they may be able to carry out some of the monitoring themselves. Monitoring usually looks at the following:

1 Access and image
   • how easy is it to get to the library?
   • the outside 'appeal'
   • access to the inside
   • internal 'appeal'
   • accessibility throughout the library for wheelchairs, pushchairs or for people with a disability, etc.
   • readability of notices
   • guiding to the various areas of the library.
2 Safety
   • the condition and safety of furniture and equipment
   • health and safety
3 Staff
   • evidence of a corporate policy
   • the ability to deal with complaints
   • evidence of community involvement
   • staff skills and appearance
   • staff relationship with users
   • how staff help the user when answering an enquiry
   • staff training
4 Stock
   • evidence of stock work
   • appearance, order and arrangement of stock
   • position, accessibility, etc., of the library catalogue
   • availability, location, height, etc., of IT facilities.

Many of these items are relevant to children's work, and can provide valuable information for the development of the service.

Quality monitoring is well advanced in a number of areas including Westminster and Berkshire, where both authorities take a whole service approach rather than a special monitoring process for the children's service. This ensures that the children's service develops alongside whole library provision. It is perceived as part of the whole library service, not 'special' or an 'add on' as often happens elsewhere.

Comments and suggestions from children

All citizens should have the right to complain about or comment on the services available to them. Many authorities have general complaints procedures, but few have specific provision for children's responses.

Cambridgeshire has created an excellent example of such a procedure by imaginatively using Asterix illustrations and text style. It is headed:

> By telling us what you think about the library, you will help us get it right.

The form asks:

- Do you enjoy coming to the library? Tell us why
- Are there things you really like about the library ? Tell us what
- Are there things you really don't like about the library? Tell us what
- Are there books you would like more of in the library? Tell us which

Leading quality

There are some key issues the manager must always remember if s/he wishes to lead the library service towards a better future:

- throw aside the negative and concentrate on the positive
- nothing is so sacred that it should not be examined anew
- decisions should be taken firmly when and where needed
- staff and users should be kept informed as to what is being done, why and with what results
- any change should be facilitated smoothly
- look beyond current objectives to future plans, however far ahead
- aim to be as good a leader as humanly possible for as much of the time as possible
- if leadership is the fulcrum of the library service, the user is the lever.

References

1 Cross, G., *The dark behind the curtain*, Leamington Spa, Scholastic, 1995.
2 Mark, J., *Thunder and lightnings*, Harmondsworth, Puffin, 1976.
3 Blanshard, C. (ed.), *Children and young people: Library Association guidelines for public library services*, 2nd edn, London, Library Association Publishing, 1997.

Part 2
Setting the strategies

6
Strategic management

'The library doesn't keep books in alphabetical order any longer,' I told her. 'The children's section is all done by dots now. . .'

'The barbarians have taken over . . . Why don't they just tear down the shelves and hurl the books into four huge piles: *Boring*, *All-right*, *Dead good*, and *Brilliant.*'

A. Fine, *Goggle-eyes*[1]

Service strategies

Having assessed current provision for children from a whole library service perspective or from that of a single library; having decided what is good and bad, what needs changing and developing and where the focus needs to be; having developed the skills to initiate change, the next step is to develop strategies for each aspect of children's provision. These strategies can be determined by client group, by service type or by a combination of both. This section looks at some of the different strategies that can be developed and includes examples of possible approaches to build on.

For many children's librarians the strategies are already in place, but they may not be put in writing, and it is important that they should be. Strategies are the day-to-day reason for being here and formalizing them in writing enables you to justify the reason for the service, its impact and coverage. Strategies should fill the Tasks section of the model for service organization in Figure 1.6 (p.36).

Role and value of strategic management

Setting strategies for a service involves a constant process of planning and action, based upon reality and focused on success. In the context of any service it is necessary to examine:

- what?   the end result – the aim
- how?   means of achieving the aim

- why?   the philosophy
- where?   where the activity will take place
- who?   the people involved and their roles
- when?   the timing.

Strategic management is valuable for a number of reasons. Amongst these, it:

- sets a clear direction
- provides a long-term vision
- provides a clear, defensible base from which staff may make local decisions
- improves performance by clearly defined targets and measures
- can incorporate rapidly changing circumstances
- builds teamwork and expertise
- makes the aims and action of the service visible to all staff
- encourages creativity and innovation by setting clear aims for service delivery
- challenges assumptions
- ensures efficiency and effectiveness and identifies the value the service adds.

These general principles of strategic management are very useful in creating a framework for the development of strategies for different aspects of the children and young people's service. If you work through the different questions and gain an understanding of the benefits, you will be able to create really effective strategies. These can then be used to measure performance and therefore success. It is possible by this means either to create a strategy for the whole young people's service, or to break it down into its natural segments of age groups or specific need.

If you break it into these elements, you will have the key constituents of the business plan which is outlined in Part 1, and tasks or strategies can be formulated around the following key building blocks:

- under-fives
- children's service
- teenage service
- special needs

- activities
- IT
- information.

While there is some obvious overlap, the related services follow the accepted child development milestones. Strategies for each of these sectors are invaluable and, when added to the overall purpose, values, staffing and quality management programmes described in Part 1 they build into an effective business plan.

The business plan must be a working document which will grow, develop and change over the coming months and years. It is usually made up of strategy statements and an annual action plan with development targets. Overall strategy statements can be written for each aspect of the library service to ensure that staff know what the aims are for the total service. While a great deal of work goes into their initial production, they will not need re-writing every year but will become the base document from which an annual action plan and targets can be created. The approach of every authority will be different. What follow are some of the issues for the children's service today, written in the form of strategy statements. They are unlikely to be in any one authority's house-style nor to cover all activities, but they form a basis upon which a business plan can be built.

An under-fives' service strategy

Purpose
To provide all under-fives and their carers with high quality library services and to ensure that these services are readily and easily available to them.

Objectives
Examples of objectives that may be identified are:

- To create an exciting service for the individual child
- To provide resources and an environment which stimulates and educates youngsters
- To empower the under-fives to develop social, participative and manual skills by providing activity and story sessions

- To implement the Children Act by providing as far as possible a safe and secure environment and ensuring that carers are notified of their responsibility
- To address the needs of the specific groups created to serve this age group and their carers
- To provide these groups with a service either by their visiting the library or by the library service visiting them
- To engender a love of books, reading and libraries.

The customers of the service

This is a unique group for the library service, as the main target, the child under the age of five, is usually beholden to an adult for allowing her/him access to library provision. The customers are, therefore, wide-ranging and include:

- under-fives
- parents and carers
- childminders
- parent-toddler groups
- pre-school playgroups
- voluntary nursery schools
- maintained nursery schools
- special needs and opportunity groups
- care groups and social services.

Each library should know of the approximate population of under-fives it serves and of the groups within the community.

Library design

All service points, including mobiles and trailers, should have a section of stock dedicated to the needs and interests of the under-fives age group and their carers. The larger libraries should have an area that is specifically designed, furnished, stocked and guided for under-fives. There is a great deal of attractive furniture now available ranging from colourful eye-level shelving to specially designed 'kinder boxes' which can take the form of such objects as trains and fire engines. The area should be carpeted, there should be child-level seating and bean bags, soft bouncy seating or large soft toys.

One area of design where most libraries fail is in the provision of toilets. Use of staff toilets by young children causes much concern amongst staff. Unless toilets can be provided, a clear policy on access to staff facilities should be agreed with staff representatives.

Stock

Each library should provide a wide range of stock, including board books, picture books, 'beginning to read' material, early development toys for use in the library, resources for carers, cassettes, videos, CDs and CD-ROMs. The stock should reflect the multicultural society of today and should avoid sexist and other offensive images. There should also be a collection of interactive stock for those children with learning or manipulative difficulties.

An area or authority-wide stock policy for this group should be established. It is the major area of stock subject to seasonal variation, aggravated by potentially heavy issue to groups. There should be adequate stock to serve all groups in each area.

Budget

Because this is the only section of a library the under-fives can use, combined with the high wear-and-tear and high cost of the material, a significant proportion of the materials budget must be dedicated to under-fives' needs. In many regions a minimum of 30% of the young people's budget for each library should be allocated to develop and maintain stock for the under-fives.

Activities

A range of activities should be organized for this age group. These should be interactive and based firmly on library resources. They should involve stories to develop listening skills and enjoyment of story, rhythm and rhyme as an introduction to the world of children's literature. Story times should not just be held 'for the sake of them': their content and timing should be discussed with the local community to find the most suitable arrangements. (For more details see the section on 'Literacy' on pages 143–8).

Security

Child security is very important and The Library Association's guidelines for unsupervised children[2] are recommended for adoption by all authorities in the United Kingdom (see Appendix). Elsewhere, the availability of national guidelines should be investigated. Clear notices should be provided for all libraries reminding parents or carers of their responsibilities. Further advice should be given to staff about dealing with difficult or threatening circumstances.

In society today there is a growing concern for the safety of very young children following a number of unpleasant incidents. Librarians must be sensitive to this concern in the layout of their libraries. Consideration should be given to the introduction of video monitoring in children's libraries which are either in a separate room or fairly isolated by tall shelving. If these are constantly staffed, however, simple panic alarms may be all that are required. Panic alarms are also a good idea in rooms where activities take place. Small children tend to treat dark spaces such as under stairs, behind photocopiers, etc. as exciting, adventurous caves, until they get stuck or frightened. It is important to look at the whole library from a very young child's perspective and to be aware of the problem. The Library Association guidelines for unsupervised children provide more detail about security and layout issues.

Service to groups

Libraries should consider how groups of young children are able to use the library. Much depends upon the way groups are organized in the country concerned. In the United Kingdom changes in nursery provision and the introduction of trading, whereby some school library services must now sell their service to schools, have made support arrangements complicated. Every group should have equal access to the library, but this might be as individual users. Provision needs careful planning because the bulk loans can strip small libraries of much of their resources. Often these loans do not add much to issue figures unless the authority has a formula for calculating them. This may not be a problem, but it needs considering. In some regions provision is split between schools library services and public library services, with school library services serving those for-profit institutions such as nurseries. Public library services support playgroups, parent-toddler groups and childminders. For those using the public library service access could be by means of:

- formalized loans from community libraries to groups within their catchment area

- adequate exchange facilities
- community contact with specialist staff at community libraries by means of activities, visits and talks with under-fives
- a service for childminders.

A major step forward for some authorities to encourage support would be a reassessment of the statistics recorded for service to these groups. Alternatively, with rapidly decreasing budgets and increasing issues it might be decided not to encourage bulk loans but to encourage visits to the library where the children join as individuals. The concern here is that this depends upon an enthusiastic leader with the time and energy to organize the trips. At least children in groups can interact with books without the leader being a 'book' person.

Targets
Once a strategy has been written to cover these and other locally relevant points, measurable targets need to be set to ensure that the service improves. The targets will be linked to local circumstances but are likely to cover some of the following:

- Improve quality and quantity of stock in all libraries. All stock to meet targets for age, turnover, condition and coverage within two years.
- Create community profiles for all libraries to indicate numbers of children and number and types of groups within the community.
- Ensure that under-fives' stock equals at least 20% of the children's library and is funded by 30% of the budget.
- Maintain an annual survey of groups and an annual promotion to new groups in each community area.
- Implement the Children Act, or its equivalent, as it relates to libraries.
- Maintain the service to childminders, attracting new childminders.
- Investigate the possibility of introducing toy libraries; develop an implementation plan by the end of the year.
- Develop jointly with education and social services provision of an early years information service for parents and carers. Plan in year one, fund and begin implementation in year two, complete implementation in year three.

These targets will be monitored and evaluated annually and reset as part of the development plan.

Children's services strategy

Purpose
To provide all children of primary school age, and their parents and carers with a high quality library service, readily and easily available to them.

Strategy statement
This part of the service is probably the most heavily used but the least analysed or managed. The same approach can be used for the primary school age range as for the under-fives, as many of the issues for consideration are the same, although the answers may be different. The customers and objectives of the service need to be defined and issues which affect design and security need to be clarified. An indication of the budget and an activities strategy are also vital. Other areas for consideration are literacy development and support for the National Curriculum, both of which are followed up later in Part 3. When developing a strategy it is worth taking the opportunity to challenge some typical assumptions, particularly about stock, and these are what are considered now.

Questions to ask

Non-fiction

- Is it still reasonable to expect all libraries to cover all non-fiction subjects? Non-fiction buying should be analysed and possibly reduced, because not all non-fiction is being borrowed. Should public libraries be concentrating on leisure reading and the needs of the National Curriculum? Or should they just cover leisure? Are there better ways of providing homework support, for example short loan collections? What areas could be discontinued by all libraries – or just by small libraries?
- How can delivery be made less cumbersome and less prohibitive? How can we make it easier for children to find what they want, for example subjects such as pollution and conservation, history and exploration.
- Would some subjects such as poetry have more impact if they were shelved in separate sections? Or does this lead to confusion?

- Would staff efforts be better spent looking at how non-fiction is promoted, not only in terms of display but in terms of how it is promoted to groups and how the skills are taught?
- What sort of guiding would be appropriate?
- For whose benefit is there a junior reference collection?

Fiction

- The ability to read requires a range of skills and when a library selects stock it should be appropriate to acquiring and developing these skills. Are categories of stock helpful to the child and his/her carer or are they just for the benefit of the shelver? Should the categories of stock used be in relation to reading ability or to theme of book? If the latter, does this turn the child into a genre reader at too young an age? Is enough being done to promote some picture books as reading books? Are libraries too heavily driven by format in categorization of stock?
- Reading for pleasure and enjoyment requires a range of stock, but is there the right balance between key authors and books that are hyped elsewhere?
- Why will some people buy books in supermarkets but not borrow them from a library? What is putting them off? How can we learn from what supermarkets do differently?
- Does the series approach that most publishers take to younger readers drive selection? If so are we encouraging reading to formula? Does it matter?
- What is the right balance between hardback and paperback? Is enough being bought of each? Should both be available in all sizes of library?
- Should fun books and older picture books be separated from the rest of the fiction by creating another category?
- How can IT be capitalized upon to attract more users but still be used appropriately? Children need to know how to assess when it can be helpful and when it is inappropriate to use.

Stock management

- Is a sufficient percentage of the budget being spent on this age group?
- What type of stock performance targets should be set?

- What is the age and condition of the stock?
- What percentage of total stock holding is for this age group?
- What percentage of child membership is within this age group?
- How much non-fiction as opposed to fiction do they borrow?
- All stock should reflect the diverse needs of contemporary, multicultural society. Is enough stock being bought to raise awareness in ethnocentric areas? Are libraries promoting this stock sufficiently?

Services for young people

Aims
To provide and promote a wide range of high quality resources, meeting both the short and longer term information and leisure needs of teenagers.

Objectives

- To provide an accessible, defined library environment which will attract this client group into the library.
- To provide a specialized information service to teenagers, with particular emphasis on current local and national needs or trends.
- To promote the library as a source of relevant information and as a gateway to other information providers.
- To promote reading at a time when many interests compete for teenagers' time.
- To organize events inside or outside the library which will promote the services the library provides, liaising with other agencies as appropriate.
- To make available, where appropriate, resources and services in alternative locations which already provide youth and community services to teenagers.
- To involve young people in the development of the service.

Customers
A literal definition of youth library customers would be those aged between 13 and 19. In practice the age span could range from 12 to 25, with all that that implies in terms of rapidly changing needs as young people move through the age range. A community profile is thus essen-

tial to assess local needs according to population. In practical terms, resources in libraries for this group fall into two categories:

Teenagers	11/12–14
Young adults	15–19.

For these groups in particular, there is a high proportion of potential as well as current users. The Public Library Review[3] research found that 16 and 17 year-olds are the most frequent users of libraries amongst those over the age of 14, visiting a library on average over 20 times a year. In Warwickshire three out of four teenagers use the library. In Birmingham 16–18 year-olds use the library more heavily than any other age group.

Stock

A wide range of media is particularly important to attract and maintain the interest of this client group and should include a high percentage of paperbacks, magazines, cassettes, compact discs, videos, CD-ROMs and leaflet material. It is crucial that stock reflects current trends and fashions, so a higher proportion of ephemeral material than is usually stocked in libraries is required. Aslib's public library research[3] showed that 80% of teenagers use libraries for study or information for living. In most cases GCSE and vocational type material is housed in the adult library and signposted from the teenage collection. The introduction of homework collections to support the National Curriculum and GCSE study may change this policy, or may lead to some duplication of stock. For further details on homework support see Chapter 9.

Collections can be circulated between libraries in order to provide a regularly changing bookstock. This provides maximum value by ensuring a rapid turnover of standard titles and keeping stock fresh.

Library environment/design

Where space permits, each library should have a defined area for teenage and/or young adult provision. The background environment should be modern: furniture and equipment should be bright and there should be maximum face-on display. Provision of audio and multimedia facilities is essential.

It may be desirable to actively explore the possibility of siting young adult collections in centres already used by young people.

Budget

Finance needs to be provided both from children's and from adult funds, as teenage needs span both these areas of library provision. At least 2% of adult funds should be allocated to youth collections, and in fact where the community profile is higher the budget should be in proportion. Discussion on allocation should involve both adult and children's staff in order to provide a coordinated, cost effective approach.

Activities

Community libraries have held very successful activities and promotional events for the youth client group, promoting reading, leisure and information provision. Links with other agencies such as schools, youth groups and other information providers have proved especially worthwhile in contributing to the success of events. These links should be maintained and strengthened. Promotional activities at venues other than the library could be further investigated.

In Cheshire, for example, targeted library visits focus on help with GCSE information skills through fun workshops entitled 'The library under siege'. Young people are involved in role-playing characters who are only able to progress by using information sources within the library.

Staff training

Some library staff may feel uneasy about contact with the youth client group. Consideration needs to be given as to whether staff training in this area requires updating, and whether it would be a good idea to incorporate it in staff induction programmes so that the matter becomes less of an 'issue'. Young people are entitled to be treated with respect and to have their enquiries and needs taken seriously.

Service to groups

In many cases libraries have made positive contact with appropriate organizations such as youth groups. Consideration should be given to the provision of collections of materials to such groups, particularly with regard to aspects such as finance, security, etc. Personal contact with groups will keep a service's profile high and will enable library staff to keep in touch with the current needs of teenagers. A bright, relevant poster should be designed to publicize library services to these age groups.

The type of support given by the public library service to schools needs careful definition. The extent of support will depend upon other provision within the area. Does the school have a library? Is there a schools library service? Does the school have its library budget delegated to it from the local authority or does it have private funds? Where there is a schools library service it is vital to devise a clear statement of what is available to the school from each of the services in order to avoid confusion or exploitation. Such a statement has been produced by a number of authorities such as Bedfordshire and Cambridgeshire.

Marketing strategy

It is essential to clearly identify the market segment, establish which unique services and resources the library can provide more effectively than can other agencies and then target these areas. Much work has already been done in assessing customer needs. This now needs to be applied to service developments.

When developing a marketing strategy it is also worth working in conjunction with schools library services to develop contact with the client group through schools, in order to promote provision and keep alert to changes in client group needs. Publicity should be constantly reviewed, as should how and where it is distributed. The aim should be to continually market in different or unusual places and use different approaches so as to change negative images.

Information provision

The right to know is the reverse coin of the ability to learn how to learn. An area which many libraries have failed to tackle so far is that of the information needs of young people. One of the reasons for this may be the library working ethic of non-intervention. If we allow this philosophy to dominate, then as a consequence the library will remain the place to which young people don't come for information, even though it is the place which is most likely to provide what they need.

The nature of information provision in libraries must change as rapidly as the needs and desires of society change and expand. Unless this challenge is tackled, libraries will be left with a mass of broad-based, generalized and unfocused information, much needed but little used. Material is too often found behind desks, filed in a retrieval system and boxed because it is flimsy. In this situation it takes real dedication on the part of staff to manage information and it takes real persistence on the part of the reader to find it.

None of this really fits the nature of many of today's young people. They know they want information. At a recent conference on the information needs of young people[4] a mixed audience of youth workers and librarians was addressed by young readers who pleaded for their right to access information. They asked 'why young people had to go to adults to get what they want, especially as adults say they want to listen but they do not act on what they hear'. The young people wanted information created by young people, and someone to talk to as well as information in leaflet form. They wanted to browse, not to have to ask. One teenager closed the conference by saying,

> I know many people like myself are in situations that they really don't know where to turn. I hope that the wide range of teenagers who feel that there is no one to turn to will soon be a minority. So I ask you to please listen to young people as only they can say what they need.

Information is a key to library's future, as is the technology which provides it. Libraries are very good at acquiring and organizing information but we need to be better at making it accessible. There is a huge niche begging for us to fill it and take control. But, if we do, we have to make radical changes to our information sections. We may need to duplicate, target and certainly not shelve spine-on. This information is often in leaflet form and is thin and flimsy and soon 'gets lost' if shelved in traditional way. Face-on display allows users to browse and find what they are looking for without having to ask.

A number of libraries have made inroads into this challenge. Bromley are a fine example of this with their shocking pink 'Upfront' teenage sections and their impressive fact files, which have changed users' views that libraries are not 'hip' or 'cool'.

Hertfordshire have built on Bromley's experience by creating 'Factfiles' of information with its information logo. The files are quality stamped by youth and community services as having reached their standard for information for young people. These will be available in every public library, secondary school library, and youth centre. The aim is for young people to become accustomed to the logo and know that if they see it they are guaranteed quality information.

It is well worth creating an information strategy for young people, particularly those at the top end of the age range. This should be integrated into the more general teenage strategy. It may be an opportunity to develop your first joint strategy with other services, for example youth and community.

A young peoples' information strategy

Aims
To create a multi-agency information web with young people at the centre, and to ensure that, wherever they are, young people will be able to gain access to all kinds of information quickly, easily and without prejudice.

Objectives
Examples of objectives that may be identified are:

- To ensure that all organizations involved work together to provide information in a cohesive form
- To create a common 'look' so that young people anywhere within an authority can identify an information source, and all have access to the same information
- To create a database of relevant information on local events and activities, which also provides a gateway to more ephemeral or less targeted activities for those with more specialist interests
- To network the database throughout the authority to places in which young people naturally congregate, such as clubs, infoshops, schools, libraries, street corners, their own and others' homes
- To develop mobile cyber centres to provide young people with further opportunities to access information
- To create a booklet, both paper-based and as a Web site, which signposts young people to useful addresses and agencies on a wide range of issues and covering a multitude of needs
- To train young people in the skills required to handle all types of information
- To involve young people in the development of information.

Organizations working together
In any type of authority a number of organizations have been identified

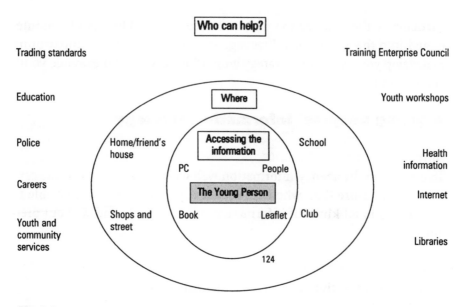

Fig. 6.1   *Young peoples' information web*

as providing information to young people. It is possible to build up an information web or network of all of these organizations working together. To create the infrastructure it may be appropriate to bring together just those that are seen as the key players. Examples of these are: the Training Enterprise Council (TEC); careers services and health information services (may be called health promotion services). Alternatively this strategy may be initiated jointly by library and youth and community services before gradually bringing in other organizations.

Common image

Working with young people on a common image for the authority is a good place to start. This image should be used in youth and community centres, in libraries and in schools. In the United Kingdom the National Youth Agency has taken the lead in developing a Youth Information database for national data and has introduced symbols which categorize the information section in their information shops. This image could be incorporated into the database graphics, and as organizations join the network/web they should be encouraged to use it. It is recommended that the image is made up of graphic logo and text style which can be used together or separately. This would provide the opportunity for local young people to be involved in naming their local collection, in order to ensure that local people feel they own the collection. They would use the pre-agreed text style on the signs and guiding to maintain an authority-wide approach.

Common information

Youth information shops provide an extensive range of information and access to counselling. Libraries should find out whether there are any of them available in their neighbourhood. Even better, information shops housed within libraries, as in Mansfield Library, have proved a great success. While it is highly unlikely that information shops can be completely replicated in libraries throughout an authority it is possible to identify the core material necessary to set them up.

This smaller core collection can then be made available in sites around the authority, thus making information easily accessible to young people without them having to ask for advice. If there are strong links between the public library service and the schools library service, it may also be possible to introduce this core information into schools under the same logo. This smaller core must always relate to the more extensive collections in Information Shops.

Database

The Nottinghamshire 'Town Crier' system and the Hertfordshire database, InfoCentre, are examples of an ideal base for the development of local information. They contain records of organizations, clubs, groups and societies, many of which are relevant to young people and often have the capacity for a 'what's on' section. The National Youth Agency has also launched an excellent database of national information sources which is not only valuable for personal use by young people but ideal for GCSE and NVQ studies. The ultimate aim would be to combine local and national data, thus creating a huge resource for young people. Available on the Internet with 'in your face' graphics, the impact could be stunning.

If this system was available in local clubs and youth and community centres, with the facility to edit and be built on by local young people, it would become truly relevant to local needs. With high specification computers, the whole project could be fronted by attractive and appropriate graphics, again designed by young people. The aim would be to achieve computer access, either as a standalone touch screen unit or as a multi-use computer, to all types of venues where young people congregate such as fast food outlets, clubs and the street corner.

A number of schools are currently setting up young business schemes, and many of these incorporate an IT interest. It may be possible to support some of these who are working on database development or website work.

Mobile cyber centres

Young people have limited opportunity to move around to static sites of information. In many areas, if the service wishes to reach the majority of young people, it needs to become mobile. This is an opportunity for a joint project with the schools library service to create a dual use small mobile cyber centre. Such a vehicle could be used during the day for attending schools, and in the evenings for visiting various venues known to be meeting points of young people. Fitted out with: detachable shelving; computers with word processing, Internet and InfoCentre; leaflets and reference material; fiction; a coffee machine and easy seating, such a meeting place may provide for some young people their first access to information.

If the library service is unable to finance such a venture, it should check out what mobile provision the local youth service has available. Often it has acquired an old single-decker bus for visiting particularly difficult urban and rural sites in the evenings, or it may have a sex or drugs information bus. Whatever the provision, the library service should get involved. It may be feasible to provide quick reference material and some popular fiction by this means. There is also the possibility of providing telephone back-up support to these mobile vehicles when the local static library is open, so that young people or their counsellors can ring to ask for information, or even to reserve an item which might be of use to a young person. Such cooperation is the very basis of developing good links with young people. Unfortunately many libraries close just as youth work is beginning. All too often poor telephone communication can become a problem in libraries. The service needs to think more positively if it is to have a chance of successfully tackling the information needs of young people.

Static cyber centres

Mission
To work alongside young people of about 13–19 to provide a 'Cybercafé'-

style Internet facility that is 'owned' by them. The project will enhance IT opportunities that will enable them to access information from many sources and to develop the skills needed to exploit it.

Objectives

- To work alongside young people to identify and meet their specific information needs.
- To enable contact to be made with other young people throughout the world, to discuss common issues and gain an understanding of differences between them.
- To provide professional support and guidance, if required, by young people, in a safe, age-group-related environment.
- To close the gap between the information-rich and the information-poor.
- To give young people support in meeting their information needs.
- To enable young people to develop the skills to use the Internet.
- To develop IT skills such as word processing, desktop publishing and creation of spreadsheets.
- To provide opportunities for young people to develop information-handling skills, encompassing a wide range of sources from reference books and leaflets to CD-ROMs and beyond.
- To provide a facility in which young people can have *fun*, learning from and experimenting with new technology.
- To investigate how technology can extend the current methods of information provision.
- To give access to any existing database of local clubs, groups, organizations, etc.

In the long term it is worth assessing the feasibility of extending use to other members of the public. This is to enable young people to develop relationships with adults where the young people may take the lead and where the environment may be particularly supportive. If a new centre is feasible it should have disabled access. There should be an easy seating information area and a quiet area for confidential counselling support. Alternatively the local council may be able to put in a free telephone line between venues, for example to the nearest youth information shop, in order to provide these advantages.

The technology offered should include a range of CD-ROMs, word processing, spreadsheet facilities and Internet access. A useful addition to provision is a big screen mounted above the PCs. This will discourage young people from accessing pornography. It will also encourage learning to be shared. The cost of access to equipment can be prohibitive, and, where possible, a free first half-hour would offer a huge benefit to young people. A charge could then be made for further access and for Internet use. Charges can usually be made for printing. Ideally smart-card technology could be developed which would provide the means for charging young people for access. This can be linked to personal computers in order to activate extended use. It would also enable discreet support to be offered to those young people who are disadvantaged in any way.

Such a centre should aim to be at the forefront of technology, and considerable thought should be given to the installation of such systems as CD-i. A decision on whether to install games is also needed from the outset, because it sets the theme for the venue. Local industry often sees these venues as a way of working with the community, particularly if they have an IT base. It may be possible to develop arrangements whereby companies either donate good equipment, site their systems in the centre, or offer staff to share their expertise with young people. Staffing of such centres is crucial, and where possible they should be staffed by both library staff and youth workers. Both must be interested in the technology on display and be able to communicate with the users. As the basic aim is to access information there may be some need for counselling support, so links to the information shop and to youth workers available for rapid intervention are vital.

Depending upon space, funding and relationships with other services, it may be possible for a library service to provide some or all of these features. It will thereby attain and maintain a position at the cutting edge of developments in youth librarianship.

How to evaluate success
The success of such a centre should be measured in the following terms:

- usage, for example patterns of usage, numbers, user profile
- what areas are most used – IT equipment?
                                – information?
                                – support?

- the ability of the centre to keep up with it developments
- downtime of equipment.

Information handling skills

It is vital that young people develop the skills of handling information so that they can gain maximum benefit from it. This skills teaching is now a fundamental part of the National Curriculum and where there are school librarians they are constantly helping young people to develop the necessary skills. Pages 131 and 175 investigate information skills and the impact of the Internet on information handling.

Involving young people

Involving young people in decision-making is vital. They are very clear what is important to them. Brian Thompson, a young person invited to close the Youth Information Conference already referred to,[4] said:

> Young people don't need people in suits taking away control or making fun of them. I ask that when you return home you try to encourage and inspire young users and colleagues alike to pressure local decision makers to talk and listen to the younger generation and press for the implementation of suggestions and proposals.

> If we are to achieve the worthwhile goals it is young people who must identify what their needs are and how we should provide and present the information. Youth empowerment is an empty achievement without youth voice.[4]

> Bear in mind the following statements from an oriental philosopher:

> Tell me and I forget. Work with me and I know. Involve me and I understand.

If we take these comments on board, weaving a web of involvement, then we shall have laid the foundations to build on.

Young people are very keen to be involved in the development of projects for which they are the intended audience. Projects which involve young people can be hugely effective and often have an impact far in excess of that anticipated. Too often librarians stand by the principle of 'we know best', or are concerned that they are somehow diminishing the profession by allowing others to become involved. Try it, look at the results and judge for yourself. Experience has taught that the benefits hugely outweigh that little bit more time that is required to work with others. For further discussion of this, see 'Children as active partners in decision-making' on page 54.

If young people are to be involved then there must be a real role for them. They could be given the bookfund budget and taken to a library supplier, they could work with a shelving contractor to choose the design and layout of the furniture, they could name and design the logo, or they could paint the mural. All these projects invariably produce stunning results for both the young people and for the librarians involved. Even better, they could form a management committee or user group. As such they are eligible to apply for grants and National Lottery funding, they may attract the interest of The Prince's Trust; many people are willing to offer sponsorship to support projects organized by young people. There is a great sense of achievement for all involved, superb publicity can result and the final outcome is truly customer-driven.

A word of warning

When deciding what steps to take to meet the information needs of young people, the types of information to be covered must be thought through. The young people at the information conference already referred to,[4] told the audience what they wanted: materials on emotional issues, sexual issues, drug-related issues, etc, and primarily information produced by other young people. They said 'you may be surprised and it may embarrass you, but this is what we want and need'.[4] As mentioned earlier, public library review research and that carried out in Birmingham reinforced this view. The success of youth councils in a number of local authorities has given young people a strong voice and they are continually demanding information.

Making this information high profile and easy to access – without young people having to ask for it – means that it may raise issues for other readers or with young people's parents. This should not become a reason to abandon the policy, but it does need careful management. All staff need to understand the aims and purpose of youth provision and be able to respond to queries or complaints. The material should not be placed too near the young children's section and should be clearly labelled for its audience. The creation of information fact files with covers designed by young people, which have proved so successful in

Bromley, is one way of tackling the situation. The need for this information and its ease of access is the uppermost issue but it should be managed in all libraries to avoid unnecessary complaint.

Targets

Targets need to be set for service to young people. Some examples of activities which need to be measurable are:

- The establishment of a pilot young adult library to provide a 'model', which can be evaluated and lead to further developments.
- The development of an approach to information provision targeted at young people.
- The assessment of staff training needs in relation to the client group, and the instigation of a training strategy.
- Finding a new name to replace the undesirable 'teenage services' perhaps by promoting a competition in school/community libraries?
- Undertaking a major review of teenage stock with full financial implications.
- The improvement of links with teenagers through contact with schools, youth groups, school library services and other agencies.
- A review of information provision for teenagers with proposals for improvements.

A special needs strategy

Purpose

To provide for all children the opportunity to exploit the resources available through the public library, and to consider the eradication of factors which prevent this happening.

Objectives

Examples of objectives that may be identified are:

- To create an exciting service accessible to as many young people as possible.
- To ensure that a match between resources provision and user need is achieved through the provision of material appropriate for linguistic/cultural background or special need provision.

- To address issues of the accessibility of libraries for people with special needs.
- To provide a service at both the local library and at centres for children with special needs.
- To engender a love of books and an awareness of the information potential of the public library.

Customers of the service

The terms 'special services' or 'community services' cover a huge range of potential clients. There is much debate on the acceptable names for different ethnic groups, illnesses and disabilities. The use of the wrong one can cause great offence. Linking them all under one heading of 'special needs' is also unacceptable to many, but it has been used here for simplicity. This is just one approach, but the vital first step for any authority is to find out what is acceptable locally. Services include provision for:

- minority ethnic groups
- cultural minorities, including travellers
- those with physical disabilities such as loss of hearing, loss of vision, etc.
- those with mental illness
- those with learning difficulties
- children with disabilities
- children in hospitals
- those working with social services, care groups, etc.

Information on groups and individuals with special needs in the community can be rather vague and non-statistical. Help may be available from the planning or housing department, from community groups such as your local disability information service, or from the education department. The acquisition of this type of information is likely to be a long-term project, and will require the development of close working relationships within the community.

Library design

Levels of service provision for young people with special needs must be determined. Should stock be separate or integrated? Shelved or boxed?

Should all special needs material be grouped together, regardless of the need? Should material be kept exclusively for the use of 'special needs' children? Issues relating to provision for minority ethnic communities, including guiding, minimum stock level, stock exchange, where material should be shelved, etc. need also to be determined. Design and layout should also take account of cultural and physical factors to exploit potential usage such as wheelchair access. Provision on any mobile libraries needs also to be considered.

Furniture and equipment provision must consider the particular needs of the disabled young people who might wish to use the service. The Centre for the Child in Birmingham has tackled many of these issues imaginatively and services can learn much from what has been achieved there. Tables and chairs which can be altered easily to accommodate wheelchairs; a carefully designed layout to ensure that the whole section is easily accessible to all disabled youngsters or carers; and equipment such as reading machines and computers to enable them to make full use of the stock are just some of the aspects to be considered. The Library Association children's guidelines go into more detail, as do the national guidelines, *Library and information services for visually impaired people*.[5]

Stock

Stock provision for minority ethnic groups and young people with special needs has developed in a rather haphazard, ad-hoc fashion. Consideration should be given to:

- IT
- parent tongue materials
- dual language materials
- large print books
- large format books
- Braille material
- tactile books
- board books
- lift the flap material
- visual stimulus/repetitive/language development materials
- videos
- audiocassettes

Selection criteria must be developed locally for this material. There are at least two schools of thought as to quality of stock for minority ethnic groups. Some think original material should be stocked even though the general look, paper quality and binding are very different from other books in the library. Others think that children should be able to read books in their own language but in productions of the same look and quality as indigenously produced material. The growth in dual language books and translations has helped, but close liaison with each community group is the key to developing a local strategy.

Budget

The budget for community service provision needs to take into account community profiles covering such areas as language needs. Again the question is raised as to whether there should be a separate fund for special needs, or whether it should be integrated into the whole service budget and a clear buying policy adopted.

Activities

Children from all backgrounds should be encouraged to attend as many and as varied activities as possible. Events should be organized which reflect the local community and which broaden children's experiences. Dual language storytelling has great impact, as has involvement in an activity session of a local community group, such as a paperfolding session run by local Japanese residents. Events must not be patronizing or tokenistic. Making good use of local music, dance and story theatre groups can have a huge impact. All children should be treated as individuals and welcomed to activities, and this must be remembered when planning the event – can all children benefit? Activities for special needs groups need to be developed to make them more all-inclusive. For instance, school links may encourage inviting a special unit or special school to an event at the library.

Security

It is vital that all children are protected in a safe environment. The particular requirements of special needs children must be taken into account when looking at the whole library. The aim should be to make the library a safe and accessible place for all children.

Service to groups

Groups with special or cultural needs should have equal access to library services, including contact with library staff, and activities. This should include formalized loans from community libraries to groups with adequate exchange facilities built in. Consideration should also be given to schools library service coverage of services to language bases or special schools, for example. Guidelines for what is inside/outside public library provision would be useful, and should be part of the integrated strategy.

Marketing strategy

The first stage of any marketing strategy is obviously to assess the existing markets, in this case by producing a list of groups and individuals with special needs. Some element of segmentation will then follow, which will help in determining priorities. By preparing adequate publicity, a service is enabled to progress. Much excellent research by special needs teams does exist and needs exploiting! Marketing should be done in the appropriate languages and should take into account the needs and requirements of all groups.

Targets

Targets need to be set, which may cover some of the following:

- Analyse what material is currently available on special services provision
- Review guidelines to analyse service guidance provided so far
- Send to staff in libraries a questionnaire analysing provision
- Create community profiles for all libraries to indicate the number of children with special needs, etc
- Review service provision authority-wide and produce recommendations for standardization
- Analyse the effectiveness of approvals and other methods of stock acquisition for non-mainstream material
- Involve children in service development so it truly meets their needs.

An activities strategy

Definition

'Activities' is an umbrella term for the many resource-based promotional events held within the library and the community. They are an essential, important and integral part of library services to young people. The term covers planned events organized either by library staff alone or in cooperation with other groups.

Aims
To heighten public awareness by promoting the library services available.

Objectives
Examples of objectives that may be identified are:

- To make children and adults aware of what libraries have to offer as essential primary sources of information.
- To promote the library as a place to go for stimulating, enjoyable and informal learning experiences.
- To encourage reading habits and literacy, and contribute to the development of fluent readers.
- To promote the library's community role and involve local organizations in events where appropriate.
- To provide opportunities for staff to make closer contact with young people and their carers.

Customers
Customers for activities include all young people, their parents and carers, teachers and other group leaders. Each library must have drawn up a community profile for young people in its area. The public library service must maintain good liaison with the school library services so that they get to know of any school-linked activity, thus ensuring a coordinated approach to provision.

Stock
A particular library organizing an event should be responsible for providing appropriate resources to support the event, and adequate quality and quantity of stock to satisfy subsequent demand.

Budget
A minimum of 50% of a library authority's activities budget and local arts funding should be dedicated to young people's activities. A percent-

age of this amount should be used for authority-wide events. The remainder will be used locally.

Marketing strategy

A marketing strategy should establish what the customer wants by:

- discussion with children's service staff
- discussion with young people
- discussion with parents and carers
- establishing links with other activity organizers
- creating standardized assessment criteria
- circulating these assessments to all involved staff.

The marketing strategy should also make sure that the customer knows what is on offer, through such means as:

- staff training and liaison with the publicity officer
- coordinating publicity using local and national media outlets as appropriate
- exploring new sources for publicity locally, for example, supermarkets
- using libraries for publicity purposes.

Organization

Activities are divided into three groups:

1 Local activities – locally organized, local theme, e.g. half-term events.
2 Local activities – locally organized, centrally coordinated. Cross-authority theme, e.g. summer holiday events.
3 Large-scale authority events where libraries take part.

Further discussion about actual activities can be found in the section on literacy under 'Children's activities' on page 148.

Security

Security is very important and the Library Association guidelines for unsupervised children[2] should be adopted. Clear signs should be provided in all libraries reminding parents or carers of their responsibilities. Staff should be trained in dealing with difficult or threatening circumstances.

Evaluation

It is very important that activities are continually assessed for effectiveness. A simple response form which children can fill in at the end of the event is valuable, as is taking time to talk to children involved and to their parents. Fashions and interests change, and talking to children will ensure that activities remain relevant.

Targets

The targets for an activities strategy could include:

- Agree balance between authority-wide and local events
- Establish priorities annually to identify target groups
- Decide an optimum number of events for each library
- Ensure an appropriate range of activities
- Update existing guidelines to include changes in legislation
- Generate courses to ensure high quality staff training at all levels
- Publicize to staff the resources available

Convene an annual meeting with the press officer to review and evaluate publicity.

A budget strategy

Creating a budget strategy is usually the part of the children's service that is least developed. There are many benefits of leaving the children's budget well embedded in the overall budget. The cost of separating it is usually great and certainly not to the benefit of the children's section of the service. However, some authorities, which have gone down the avenue of the client/contractor or purchaser/provider split within the organization, will have separated their budget. During this process the children's budget is often isolated, along with all other sections of service delivery.

Whatever the budget situation, isolated or integrated, it is vital that the head of the children's service has a full working knowledge of the overall cost, and that any children's specialists understand costs within their area or span of control. This is important because it helps to identify priorities, it guarantees that the services provided add value and it ensures that the children's service can be justified both in times of opportunity and in times of budget crisis.

Bookfund

This is the budget that most librarians are familiar with in detail. The increasing trend to devolve it means that staff responsible for purchasing stock often also have responsibility for bookfund management. *Investing in children*[6] sets the standard materials budget for children's services. Recommendation 8 states:

> The percentage of the total materials budget applied to services for children and young people should be determined locally and should be at least the same as the percentage of children and young people in the population served.

In trying to establish the bookfund required for an authority the following need to be taken into consideration:

- the proportion of the population aged 0–16
- the amount of wear and tear on stock – often particularly heavy in the children's library and requiring quicker replacement of stock
- average costs of the different types of resources required
- from whose budget the cost of GCSE resources is taken
- variance from any standards that elected members may have set for the pro rata number of books per person
- current usage levels.

The percentage recommended by the Library and Information Services Council is that of the total materials fund, not just of the lending budget. This can make a considerable difference for the children's service. Many authorities provide this level of percentage once reference materials and specialist collections have been top sliced. This can take a large amount out of the budget, making the percentage available for children's services a much smaller figure in reality.

Having allocated a materials fund to the children's service, either it is then devolved through the service to the buying points or passed to a central buying team. There are many pros and cons with regard to the different forms of stock selection and these are touched on in in the section on 'Funding' on page 164. In many authorities the costs of resource related furniture and equipment fall within the bookfund, but for others they are separate. This is an important aspect, especially bearing in mind the need to ensure that children's areas are kept particularly safe and secure. Both a replacement and repairs budget and an IT budget should be costed, if not included, within the bookfund.

Staffing

The staffing budget for the children's service is often contained within the total staffing budget at authority or library level. If the service has no need to separate it then it is not recommended to do so. It is, however, very valuable to have a clear understanding of the costs of children's staffing support. To achieve this at an individual library level, each member of staff should be assessed for the amount of time they spend on children's work. By its nature this will be a rough percentage and can be worked out on the following grid (Figure 6.2).

This is an extremely difficult job to do but it does give you a very good indication of the costs of the service. The results are often salutary, and, having done the work for one average library, you will be able to extrapolate for all the libraries in an authority. The information thus obtained on such issues as stock selection costs and activities costs may raise some very pertinent questions. For instance, does the cost of preparation for

Job	How to work it out	Level of staff	Total
Issue and return	Time (seconds) to issue/return one book × number of issues/returns annually worked up into number of days	Average daily salary of staff including on-costs[a]	
Shelving	Average number of hours a day to shelve	Daily salary of staff including on-costs	
Specialist input	Amount of time per week, day month, etc.	Average salary per week, day, month	
Storytime	Time per week including preparation	Salary on the same basis	
Activities	Time to prepare and deliver activities for each member of staff involved	Salary on the same basis	
Enquiries	Time an average enquiry takes × number of children's enquiries	Salary on the same basis	
Stock selection	Time to chose, order, unpack, process, catalogue for each of the members of staff involved	Salary on the same basis	
Stock editing	Time taken daily, weekly or monthly to stock edit	Salary on the same basis	
Visits to schools and other organizations	Time taken per week or year including travelling time and expenses		

etc.

etc.

[a] On costs: this means the actual salary plus the costs associated with that member of staff, i.e. superannuation, insurance, etc. The personnel department will help with this.

Fig. 6.2 *Model for costing staffing support*

activities reflect the benefits? Could the costs of selection be put into purchasing more stock?

Stationery and supplies
The children's service is a heavy user of this budget, owing to the large number of activities and storytime sessions necessary. This should be understood and adequately financed. Activities and contact with so many organizations costs a great deal in terms of pens, paper, and craft materials as well as other important equipment.

Transport
Included under this heading are: the costs of visits to playgroups and schools; of selecting stock if done from central locations; of regular meetings; and a proportion of the costs attached to use of the mobile or trailer service.

Training
Added to the budget must be the annual training costs of keeping all staff in the authority updated on the library needs of children and young people, whether this is locally or centrally organized. Consideration should be given to adding the cost of extra coverage while training sessions are taking place; however, most services are able to cope unaided while staff are away.

Sponsorship
As the public purse diminishes, libraries will look more and more to alternative forms of sponsorship. A great deal of planning is necessary in order to obtain sponsorship. To be successful, you need a prospectus to inform the prospective sponsors what you are trying to achieve, who you are targeting and what is in it for them. Some figures covering footfall or audience potential will also be useful, together with an idea of how you intend to publicize the sponsor's name. You must know who to contact within an organization, as an untargeted request will invariably be ignored. It is also best to take a strategic approach in order to ensure that different individuals representing your library are not all approaching the same organizations to sponsor different elements of the service.

The Library Association runs an excellent course on Libraries and Sponsorship led by Miranda McKearney.

Staff and training

Introduction
The provision of a library service to children will be targeted, relevant and of a high quality. This requires:

- a high degree of professionalism
- staff awareness and understanding of current library issues
- a high level of commitment
- continuous adaptation and enhancement of skills
- the acquisition of new skills.

The Library Association guidelines for children and young people[7] give a clear outline of what is needed in a staffing strategy: part is repeated here for convenience:

Knowledge and skills
The following skills must be present among the staffing resources of every authority in proportion to the client group:

- an understanding of child development, including intellectual, emotional, physical, behavioural, language and social development
- a detailed knowledge of children's books, IT hardware and software, AV, multimedia, etc.
- a knowledge of appropriate information sources and an ability to assess them
- a knowledge of educational trends, developments, terminology and local structures/patterns of organization
- a knowledge of child-related groups and organizations (i.e. schools, under-fives groups, youth clubs, etc.)
- a familiarity with contemporary children's culture
- storytelling and other performance skills
- public speaking skills, particularly with regard to talking to groups of children, teachers, parents and carers
- teaching skills to promote effective library use
- promotional skills, particularly with regard to book promotion
- an understanding of parents' expectations and in relation to their children

- personal qualities, including empathy with children and confidence in
- relating to them
- management skills
- competence in working with IT
- cultural awareness and relevant language skills.

Implications for staffing policy

The required skills have the following implications for staffing policy:

- The library needs of children must be understood and acknowledged in all policy and decision-making areas, including the work of non-public departments.
- Children should have equality of opportunity with all other client groups as far as access to library provision and services is concerned.
- All staff should be trained.
- The detailed knowledge of child development, children's literature, IT software and networks, and educational matters, necessarily implies a specialist element within the staffing structure.
- Library assistants at public service points have the majority of contacts with individual children, and should be expected to develop knowledge of readers and an awareness of stock. They should not be expected to undertake professional work, but their invaluable role should be recognized.
- An appropriate recruitment and selection policy should exist whereby the library needs of children are recognized in all public library job descriptions and employee specifications. [In the UK] note must also be taken of the requirements of The Rehabilitation of Offenders Act 1974 [and the Scottish Criminal Record Checks. (For other countries any government legislation or guidelines relating to the employment of staff working with children must be understood.)]
- Positive measures should be taken to recruit staff who reflect the make-up of the community.[7]

These points identify a clear set of competencies for the children's service which should be applied, monitored and evaluated. The head of service should know which posts have which competencies invested in them, and should continually assess the effectiveness of service provision. In order to achieve a good staffing structure which supports the needs of the children in the local community and ensures the flexibility of the service it is necessary to take opportunities presented within the wider community and develop them. In order to do this, it is necessary to pay attention to staff structure, organization and training.

An information technology strategy

The Library and Information Commission's report, *New library: the people's network* (October 1997)[8] underlines the importance of public libraries in creating a bridge between the new electronic information world and our heritage in print. It recommends that government signals its commitment to an information policy with a strong emphasis on a central role for public libraries. This should be done, amongst other objectives, by the establishment of a Public Library Networking Agency to coordinate UK-wide networking developments, and by developing appropriate partnerships between the public and private sectors to implement the public library networking plan.

Against this backdrop it is more important than ever to establish an information technology strategy for your library service.

In recent years there has been a vast increase in the range of hardware and software available for both education and entertainment. The information superhighway, electronic mailing, interactive videos, pocket computers, virtual reality, etc. are all around and it is difficult to keep up with developments. Many of these new technologies have considerable educational and leisure potential.

The library should play a lead role in IT. For years it has encouraged users to develop information-handling skills. IT is just another source of information, and librarians again hold the key to access, having the skills to exploit the information. Libraries also play an important role in achieving equality of access to IT, by helping those who cannot afford their own access. A strategy for IT needs to be extremely flexible and able to easily accommodate the many new developments continually appearing on the market.

Aims

The aims of such a strategy should cover the provision and promotion of equal access to current technology for all children, ensuring the best use is made of any available technology, to access information in all appropriate forms.

Points to consider

The strategy needs to establish the philosophy that it is not the technology itself that is the most important feature. Rather, it is the way that it can enable us to accomplish old tasks better and new tasks more easily. Many children love technology as it gives them instant feedback. The excitement of multimedia and digital networks to their users is that they are are based upon discovery. Such a method allows children to learn spontaneously, to learn how to learn, without being forced, both individually and cooperatively. Suddenly there is the perception that all the knowledge in the world is, or will be, instantly available on demand to anyone who can understand and access it.

This is a very powerful concept which offers extensive opportunities for libraries to build on what they have always provided in the past. The skills of information handling previously taught to library users are fundamentally the same as those needed to get maximum benefit from information technology. If we grasp the opportunity to sell our special skills and our role within IT, a very bright future will be secured for libraries. If we do not provide IT, and do not keep up-to-date with other developments, libraries will soon become sidelined.

The benefits

The benefits of an information technology strategy are as follows:

- IT offers opportunities for users to access a wider range of resources regardless of library size.
- It improves the relevance of the public library to the child's experiences at school.
- Many children have access to personal computers at school and being able to use them in the public library increases the relevance of the library to them.
- It speeds up and eases information retrieval.
- It provides access to a wide range of stimulating material for children with special needs.
- It attracts partners and new users.

There will, of course, be problems: initial set-up costs are high; sometimes people will not use books when they are still the best source of information; there will be some difficulties with security; and demand will swiftly outstrip the facilities available.

It is therefore essential that careful thought be devoted to why libraries wish to be involved in IT, what they are attempting to achieve, and how they will manage the problems of in-built obsolescence and huge demand.

Objectives

The objectives of an information technology strategy would need to:

- seek all opportunities to develop information skills of both staff and children
- ensure equality of opportunity for all
- use technology to encourage those groups who previously felt unable to use libraries to join their local library
- use technology to appeal to those who would not otherwise use the library
- provide a gateway to a broader range of resources
- promote an understanding of how to assess the best source to answer particular questions – book, video or IT
- involve children in the development of new services
- seek partnerships with other agencies interested in IT.

Budgets

Information technology requires careful budgeting and a clear financial plan. The lifespan of the hardware will be short and will require on-going maintenance and a replacement programme built into the budget. The software is expensive and often requires licences to use. The cost of online access to the Internet or databases depends upon access methods employed and could be as reasonable as a local telephone call. However, constant use means that expenditure soon mounts up, and costs should be carefully accounted for. The wiring capacity of the building must also be assessed. Finally, printing from the different packages in use is also quite costly.

While all this sounds negative, it should not be used as an excuse to avoid the introduction of information technology. Rather, it should be used as a framework to build up the financial arguments to ensure that any scheme being planned has a sound basis and a good chance of survival.

Security

Any system which has been set up must be secure. Children love – and are very good at – either simply hiding icons or hacking into bigger systems. Access to the public library automated system should not be possible, nor should onward access into other authority systems. Protective walls, called 'firewalls', can be built around a system to prevent access, and there are methods of locking objects on screen and blocking access to control hardware. A policy for the use of disks must also be decided before launching IT. The best solution is to make the purchase of disks solely from the library mandatory; clients would have to leave them in the library between visits or would not be able to use them again. Use of personal disks should not be allowed with library equipment, as this is the easiest way to spread viruses.

Staff training

All staff should be given training with any new technology before the service is offered to the public. Staff are infected sometimes with the same excitement as the children when finding information using PCs, and these individuals should be encouraged to pursue their interests. Some libraries become so enthusiastic that they keep the PC in the 'back room' and take enquiries to it, rather than letting the readers access it themselves. This should be discouraged. The staff need to develop skills to handle all aspects of using computers and these should become part of their day-to-day work. Training should cover:

- use and selection of CD-ROMs. See the section 'Issues to consider when selecting CD-ROM' on page 166
- searching networked databases
- any automated information provision of local information
- Internet
- word processing
- printing.

The skills developed should include first stage problem solving and confidence in finding your way around the packages.

Information skills training for users

Training should be appropriate for each age. The first skill a child should learn is how to decide the most appropriate resource to start on. Skills training should cover the automated library system and local information service, CD-ROMs – how to decide which to use and how to get the best out of it – networked databases and the Internet.

Service targets

The strategy should set targets and indicators against which to measure services. At the early stages of provision this will consist of a target for the number of machines and pieces of software available in the variously sized libraries. A target for provision to the under-fives could be included, as this is often an area of IT not covered by public libraries.

Provision for those with special needs should be specifically targeted, as technology often provides them with greater opportunities for accessing information and communicating with others. Inter-agency working and partnerships should also be encouraged, especially sponsorship, this will enable the service to expand. The use of volunteers who are 'hooked' on IT is also valuable, as such individuals are often happy to share their expertise with children. The selection of IT materials should form part of the usual stock selection guidelines, and the normal approaches apply. See the section 'Issues to consider when selecting CD-ROM' on page 166.

CD-ROMs

CD-ROMs are simply devices for storing large quantities of information, including text, diagrams, photographs, animation, video clips and sound. Each disc can store about a quarter of a million pages of text, good quality sound or animation. CD-ROM titles range from text only through to multimedia encyclopaedias.

Listed below are the benefits of using CD-ROM as specified by various National Council for Educational Technology (NCET) researchers. These points can be used for arguing the case for inclusion of CD-ROMs in library stock:

* CD-ROMs are highly motivating, and with appropriate software children as young as four can use them with a minimum of supervision
* software which presents text in spoken and written form can support second language learning
* those with more CD-ROM experience can support beginners, so

encouraging users to help each other and making interaction possible
• appropriate research strategies are needed to get the best out of CD-ROMs and these can be introduced by staff.

The information superhighway and the Internet

There is little about the Internet which is obvious or simple on first inspection. It is anarchic in structure and needs time and patience to make best use of it. This multimedia, global communication network, offering conferencing, distance learning and a rich source of information, is here to stay. How it will evolve and what it will eventually look like, as bandwidths increase and nationwide cabling and fibreoptics enable more and more data to be passed down wires to more and more people, can only be guessed at. It is an extraordinary concept, and it arrived at a time when many worldwide barriers were coming down, the Berlin Wall, for example. Use of the Internet is huge, and is growing continually at an amazing rate.

Normal methods of planning can be used in developing the section of the IT strategy covering the Internet and the superhighway, and the usual questions need to be asked: What are your aims? How much money is needed? How could your aims be achieved? What are the training implications? What is your vision? However, it is also necessary to realise that the very transient nature of the technology has also to be built into the planning process. The strategy has to evolve, and only an outline of what is hoped to be achieved can be laid out at one time.

One advantage for librarians is that they have the best developed set of skills to manage their way around the Internet. Unfortunately the equivalent of Melville Dewey has yet to emerge to give the Internet some structure, but the principles are still the same. It is the most exciting environment in which to teach information skills, and the assistance of librarians will be invaluable in developing searching routines and skills. In the nineteenth century Andrew Carnegie funded many of the first libraries to promote 'the advancement and diffusion of knowledge', and as a result had an immense impact on the spread of knowledge. The Internet could well have an even more profound effect at the end of the twentieth century.

The Internet is perpetually evolving, offering opportunities for learning about new and exciting ideas and for making new relationships with other people who share some of our common goals. Information is there to be accessed, people are there to talk to, thoughts to be shared, processes to be developed and even some fun to be had! Above all, the Internet provides an opportunity to learn. A number of people believe the Internet is the only way forward, yet others have still to be convinced.

The value of the Internet

In Hertfordshire an extensive project to assess the value of the Internet, developed jointly by the education and schools library service, has been completed. The following are comments obtained from schools:

> With the Internet though, things constantly change from one day to the next. What can be more exciting than receiving information from somewhere else in the world almost immediately or the ability to access pictures and sounds from places too far away to visit? Up to the minute information from the space shuttle, views of a comet, or Cambridge by day, the latest news from anywhere in the world, the list is endless – how can books compete with this?   Primary school

> A new way of thinking. It's not the information that is important but it's the sorting it into a meaningful way.   Secondary school

> Although the information on the Internet is more up to date and available from such a broad spectrum it is not such an efficient resource in the primary schools as a CD-ROM.   Primary school

The main use for the Internet in a library is as a resource. For children there will be problems of readability; the material is, however, up-to-date, and there is great value in developing data retrieval capability and information handling skills. One school compared the use of the Internet and the use of CD-ROM:

> We use the Internet for a different kind of learning and for gathering a different kind of information than we find on CD-ROM. Learning can be planned, controlled and easily assessed using CD-ROM. We prepare worksheets to guide children through the planning and because a suitable CD-ROM is chosen we can allow free access. The Internet is different – it can be more expensive, more frustrating, slower and there is a risk of unsuitable information getting through to children. It is also exciting, unpredictable and full of information you didn't know you wanted until you dis-

covered it. There is real potential for discovery, and children rarely have a chance to discover things their teachers or parents don't know already.

Other benefits of the Internet are increased motivation, an understanding of the 'massive expanse of information travelling around the world', and the possibility of finding an answer to almost everything.

The skills

The skills required to make the best use of the Internet are built on traditional information skills. Detail of these are given here rather than in Chapter 9 on 'Education' because use of the Internet is a new approach for librarians, but they underline the need for the same fundamental information skills to be used in a new context. Skills have to be introduced, explained and practised, then continued in greater depth year by year and subject by subject. Learning to learn is a powerful aid to improving proficiency across the entire curriculum and is the basis for information access for life. The skills required are:

- basic computer and word processing skills, especially 'cut and paste'
- how best to frame a question
- which source to use
- how to formulate a search
- which sources to reject
- how to discover answers to questions
- how to read appropriately and purposefully
- how to store information
- how to combine information with previously acquired material
- the difference between originality and plagiarism
- how to incorporate new material into an assignment
- how to make appropriate notes
- how to use a variety of styles for the final presentation
- understanding key words
- curiosity
- imagination
- patience
- determination to solve problems.

In order to develop efficient surfing on the Internet there also needs to be:

- training in the use of search engines such as Meta Crawler and Web Crawler, Alta Vista, Netscape, etc.
- training in how to build bookmarks and encourage everyone to share theirs
- assessment of how children search to gain insight into thought patterns and search strategies
- collaborative searching by family groups/groups of children of different ages and sharing between individuals.

With these key skills users of the Internet can find access to a huge amount of information quickly and efficiently. They can go back to good sites easily and, once the search strategies are understood, go quickly to new sites for new information searches.

Pornography

The problem uppermost in many people's minds is that children might access pornographic or subversive materials. As a global resource the Internet is free from any form of censorship and as such children may come across such material. In a library situation, unless there are large monitors available so that ongoing searches are visible to all, this is difficult to monitor. However, NCET and RM (Research Machines), for example, have brought together a collection of good 'sites' or addresses of information which offer an opportunity to avoid such problems, while still allowing access to a huge amount of information which has been pre-selected as valuable. 'Walled gardens' are search engines which prohibit the user exploring outside a clearly defined patch of the Internet, but so far these have not proved totally protective against bad language and sexually explicit material.

The Internet reaches across the world and is now a major communication medium. This is exciting but also means that a full range of individual personalities are 'out there', including those who occasionally cause concern. The same common sense we use in everyday life must be used on the Internet too. If it is, then the Internet is fairly safe to use.

It is often best to work with children and parents to develop guidelines to ensure the best safety awareness, but the key messages are:

- **Personal information** Never give out identifying information – home address, telephone number, credit card number or school name

– in any public messaging area like chat or user groups.

• **Provocative messages**   If you come across messages that are deliberately provocative, racist, illegal, threatening or simply make you uncomfortable, do not respond to them. If you do, you are opening up a dialogue.

• **Receiving messages**   If you receive disturbing messages, talk to your friends about it and tell your teacher or parent who should inform the service provider.

• **Is it true?**   Like newspapers, just because it is on the Internet does not mean it is true. Check the sources.

• **Meeting people**   Do not arrange to meet someone as a result of an electronic contact unless there is an adult there that you know.

Pornography guidelines for the library service

Library services should develop their own Internet pornography strategy. There should be guidelines available beside each PC or as part of the log-on script. Guidance notes should also be available for parents. Check with local schools how they are dealing with the issue and ensure that the parents' guidelines encourage discussion of pornography on the Net and the arguments against accessing it.

It is advisable to set up a system to enable children and librarians to report incidents, and to check that telecommunications links are carefully handled and network use is monitored. In libraries a large screen suspended above the Internet station, so that everyone can see what an individual is looking at, can be a definite deterrent to pornography searching and is very good for collaborative working. Clear visible checking by staff will be noticed by users and will act as a further deterent.

If staff are still worried they should check with the police station. Have a publicity plan ready with the public relations department to deal with any press issues when and if they arise.

The information superhighway

The Internet is only part of the information superhighway. As technology advances and is easier to access, video conferencing and community networks will become more of a reality. Broad band technology provides high quality communication through such means as video conferencing and collaborative work on multimedia documents and datafiles. It will provide access to scarce or unusual resources, remote access to field data such as wildlife observations and, of course, access to the Internet.

Libraries will have to make sure that they are part of this revolution in order to disseminate the new information and to be fully interactive. People with Internet access are already able to stay at home to interrogate the library catalogue and request books. Eventually they may be able to go electronically to the shelf and read the book without leaving the comfort of their armchair. For some this would be an anathema but for others it may be a enormous relief, and it may bring the use of libraries to some for the first time.

In Eindhoven in The Netherlands, a library project has been carried out entitled 'the heart of an information-rich community'. Working with Philips Netherland, the city of Eindhoven and Eindhoven's public library they have investigated possible improvements to services by the introduction of 'multimedia technologies'. The new multimedia catalogue will enable users to connect their own computers to the catalogue terminals; it will provide information on issues of special interest to the user and can talk to other users sharing the same interest; and it will help the reader find his or her way around the library through state-of-the-art design ensuring easy interaction. An Infowall providing an entertaining and interactive introduction to the library, reading tables providing access to user groups, Internet, digital magazines and e-mail, and terminals on the street were the designers' solutions to the wants and needs of the Eindhoven users, and some of these features may be found in the new central library due to open in 1997. The designers have also looked specifically at the needs of children, planning a browsing and retrieval system which provides a visual search mechanism combining hierarchical and associated relationships between subjects, very similar to the search base of many CD-ROMs.[9]

Sites

The Internet is exciting, but frustrating unless you know exactly where to look for information. There are many guides and Internet magazines in existence which will point you in the right direction, but below are a few sites to get you started (which were available at the time of going to press):

Art
• <http://rubens.anu.edu.au/>

Australian National University – a collection of 27,000 images from the 15th to the 19th century.
- <http://www.cgrg.ohio-state.edu/Newark/galleries.html>
World art resources with connections to hundreds of sites.

Maths
- <http://acorn.educ.nottingham.ac.uk/Maths/>
Shell Centre for Mathematical Education.

Science
- <http://www.wcmc.org.uk/index.html>
The World Conservation Monitoring Centre.
- <http://atlantic.evsc.virginia.edu/>
The Virginian Coast reserve long term ecological research homepage.

History
- <http://www.julen.net/aw/>
The Ancient World Web: the ultimate index of all things ancient.
- <http://www.pastforward.co.uk/vikings/>
The world of Vikings
- <http://www.maryrose.org>
The Mary Rose, raised from the sea bed in 1982, can be visited on screen.

Special needs
- <http://disability.com/>
Disability resources on the Internet.

Geography
- <http://cirrus.sprl.umich.edu/wxnet>
Weathernet is a compilation of many resources.
- <http://www.ugems.psu.edu/~owens/WWW_Virtual_Library/>
The World Wide Web Virtual Library: Meteorology
- <http://www.foe.co.uk/>
Friends of the Earth

Music
- <http://www.gprep.pvt.k12md.us/classical/index1.html/>
The World Wide Web Virtual Library: Classical Music

English
- **<http://crayon.net>**
  Create your own newspaper is very stimulating.
- **<http://www.acs.ucalgary.ca/~dkbrown/index.html>**
  The Children's Literature Web Guide, based in Canada, calls itself the Internet resources related to books for children and young adults.

The future
The Internet has enormous potential, but no one know how long it will take to fully realize it. Some feel it will become the standard way of communicating, incorporating or taking over from videos, telephone, letters, television and fax. However, equally it has the potential to implode, owing to its size and its inherently anarchic nature, and others feel that the future lies in this direction.

An integrated strategy
The first recommendation in the report *Investing in children* states that:

> Each local authority should publish an integrated strategy for delivering library and information services to meet the identified needs of children and young people throughout its area, taking into account the roles, relationships and responsibilities of the major elements in the service – the public library, the schools library service and libraries in individual schools – and involving other agencies as appropriate, e.g. further education colleges, Training and Enterprise Councils.[6]

The first step in the process of creating such a strategy is to identify the roles of the services listed in the quotation above. These are outlined in the Library Association's children's guidelines, which then go on to encourage an authority to focus on the following issues:

- children's needs with respect to books, libraries, information and the encouragement of reading
- the specific roles and responsibilities of the key partners in meeting these needs
- the advantages and benefits to be gained by all the partners from a considered and carefully implemented strategy, particularly with regard to value for money, avoidance of wasteful duplication and guarding against major needs being missed altogether
- coordination, collaboration and joint or cross agency initiatives.[7]

To be successful, the most significant aspect of the work will be consultation, dissemination and endorsement throughout the authority and within a wide range of services and agencies representing the interests of children. Different partnerships have been used in different authorities, but the most common are elected members, schools and governing bodies. More extensive strategies involve youth and community services or youth workers, voluntary organizations, community organizations, under-eights officers, education advisers and school librarians.

Creating an integrated strategy

An integrated strategy combines many of the issues outlined in the strategies already outlined. Issues that need to be included are:

- The audience.
- The needs of the children that the strategy aims to support. The Library Association's children's guidelines clearly identify the needs of children in the chapter 'The Child and the Library'.
- Key principles of service delivery – or what children can expect to get from the service. This section can be compared with any children's charter the service has produced for coverage and will include the following: children will be treated as individuals with their wishes being taken into account; they can expect to receive a service tailored to their individual needs; services will help them in the transition to adult life; services will not discriminate on any grounds and will respect the beliefs and values of all children; services will work in partnership to better meet children's needs; services will support children's rights to education and health.
- Who is providing the services? Here should be listed the major providers who are working in partnership, possibly explaining the purpose of each organization or perhaps outlining a new vision, purpose and set of objectives redefined as a result of the development of the partnership.
- What are library services providing? – and what are children entitled to? The Library Association's children's guidelines again provide a framework for this.
- How the services are going to work together. This section will probably cover resources and funding, management, involvement of users, removing barriers to the achievement of the strategy and monitoring and reviewing its impact.

• Establishing an action plan.

Barnsley, Croydon, Derbyshire, Northamptonshire, Durham, Enfield and Nottinghamshire are just some of the authorities developing integrated strategies. Ideally an integrated strategy should not stop at the school library, schools library service and the public library service to children. Norfolk is an example of an authority taking a broader approach, and has involved district councils, health authorities, police and probation services as well as education and social services. The move to create three-year development plans for under-8s services sponsored by the government will be another valuable approach to ensure inclusion of library services. The topic of working with additional partners is covered in the final section of this book.

References

1   Fine, A., *Goggle-eyes*, Harmondsworth, Penguin, 1989.
2   The Library Association, *Unsupervised children in libraries*, Guidance note, London, The Library Association, 1991.
3   Library and Information Services Council, *The review of the public library service in England and Wales*, London, Aslib, 1995.
4   *The information challenge*, National Youth Information Conference, 15th May 1996. Proceedings not yet published but paper circulated to those who attended.
5   The Library Association, *Library and information services for visually impaired people*, London, Library Association Publishing, 1996.
6   Department of National Heritage, *Investing in children: the future of library services for children and young people*, London, HMSO, 1996.
7   The Library Association, *Children and young people: Library Association guidelines for public library services*, 2nd edn, London, Library Association Publishing, 1997.
8   *New library: the people's network*, Library and Information Commission, October 1997.
9   *The heart of an information-rich community*, Witte Dame Multimedia Library Project, 1996. Contact Henk Das General, Director, The Public Library of Eindhoven, Piazza 201, 5611 AG Eindhoven, The Netherlands.

Part 3
Putting life into the service

7

Key service issues

'Do you like reading?' 'Sometimes' said Andrew 'Technical manuals and magazines. I don't like reading books unless they are funny.'

'I read so slow, I can't tell what's funny and what isn't' said Victor.

J. Mark, *Thunder and lightnings*[1]

Libraries can learn from business practices: clear structures and specifications of what is available to the user, whether child or adult; measurement of what the user actually receives; good communication systems throughout the service; and the integration of the children's service into the whole library service. Using the best of business practice, a framework or infrastructure can be built to provide a solid basis for library services. With this structure in place, a number of advantages will follow: the service can be more easily defended; the benefits will be clearer; the service will be perceived to stand on its own merits; policy and strategy can be more lucidly debated; development easily identified; and more sponsorship attracted.

Having created a strong infrastructure, the real work of children's librarianship can be built up strongly and securely. The factors that make it special will then come to the fore. It will not be possible to ignore it because people will be able to see for themselves what is being done and why, what are the benefits of the service and its wider impact on the development of the child.

This next section of the book looks at turning the business plan, the specification and the measures into reality. It looks at why libraries are so important to the development of young people and why they should be the first stop for other agencies whose remit is to support children, preferably with a view to partnership and sponsorship activities.

What are we trying to achieve?

A General Store for the curious mind and learners of all ages

Zany, Brainy, Bookstore America

A multimedia store, special activities and author visits, and story hours, projects, concerts and appearances, a shop front in bright colours, 'splashy' graphics, creating an excitement and encouragement to linger. Adult sections, birthday planning and all things to do with children.

This is not the description of a library but of a children's bookstore in America – but it *could* be describing a library. We do have some beautifully designed children's furniture and attractive libraries with exciting events. There has been a major change of image away from 'cut and paste' activities. Children's libraries are appealing to a wider audience and have in many ways undergone an image transformation.

The new generation: a report on attitudes and behaviour of primary school children[2] fills in many of the gaps not covered by the Library Power research conducted by The Library Association in 1995. It points to a new life agenda for children. Children want to be empowered to make a difference to their lives. They feel critical of commerce, government and adults generally for not doing enough to solve the problems that concern them. They are suffering from advertising and promotion 'fatigue'. It is becoming more difficult to earn their loyalty. Instead, children will reward those offering services that project a challenging, ethically-based point of view. The Report suggests that children's bedrooms have replaced the street as their adventure playground, becoming centres of multimedia activities.

Children are reading less, but they are still reading more than one book every three weeks, which reflects the average issue period in libraries. They are also reading more magazines, which raises the question of whether we have reflected this sufficiently in our stock. In recent teenage surveys done in a number of authorities,[2] the need for more magazines in libraries has been strongly brought home.

Children tend to want instant gratification, and are especially responsive to promotional ploys between the ages of seven and eight. Our change of image, subconscious though it may be, has moved publicity in many children's libraries away from reactive responses towards proactive marketing, often using the brash approaches of the media. Some authorities have even adopted the loud, clashing, fast-moving images of such advertisements as 'Pepsi Max', particularly for teenagers. This is interesting in that the 'Pepsi Max' type of advertising has created by far the highest brand awareness.

There is no doubt that children are time-demanding: they frequently tax adult patience, often to the limit. However, if we look at the situation from the child's point of view, don't children also need patience? Are they not surrounded by confusing inconsistencies? Young people need a loving and protective environment. They are easily ignored and exploited: their needs can all too easily pass unnoticed, and their voice unheard.

Work in a school in Liverpool[3] has at last identified the young person as the consumer, rather than as the product, for the first time. By involving young people in the performance management of the school, this understanding has resulted in a redefined level of service quality.

Every child is extraordinary, and needs to be in today's society. Children are expected to exercise initiative, be innovative and enterprising and respond to the challenges they encounter. Learning for today's children goes much further than the mere acquisition of information. It requires the much more complex capacity to question new information, relate it to existing ideas and then formulate new ones, in order to make sense of life experiences. Surely libraries have a role here?

Literacy

This is the topical issue of our time. Governments throughout the world are issuing mandates to improve the literacy of children, and there are many literacy programmes and systems. If you want to know more about this complex issue, there are many good texts available which look at different types of literacy, investigate reading development and discuss barriers to literacy and the development programmes designed to overcome them. In this section, some of the basic types of provision and the recent initiatives in libraries will be looked at from a literacy perspective.

Current research into brain development and how this should influence education has reinforced the importance of story-telling in the development of knowledge. We must build on this research and watch how it develops to ensure that we will be able to use the new arguments to justify the role of books and reading in the development of the child as a fully-rounded individual.

Nevertheless, before there is a rush to develop a new 'literacy programme' within the profession, librarians should look at what is already being done. While this may sound cynical, there is much more chance of success in achieving literacy if it is built on basic provision. Often, repackaging what we already do under a new label is a very good place to start in order to build new ideas from a solid platform. For some the base platform may be too basic and a new programme is the only way forward, but for others much of the basic day-to-day business has a literacy aspect. The latter approach will ensure that we have in place a literary infrastructure which has a chance of a long life expectancy. If we do not do this, the current high profile of literacy could result in a collection of loosely-linked initiatives without strong foundations.

Children's activities

Many activities organized from libraries are, or should be, based on the development of reading and other skills. They therefore form an essential part of any literacy programme.

The regular **storytime** is a fundamental building block of the children's library service. Whether books are read or told, the enrapt faces of children prove that the sessions are developing listening and visual skills, as well as the important social skills of group involvement. The best storytimes take the form of a two-way session, with opportunities for children to get involved in creative thought by telling their own stories or by communicating with others. The involvement of action rhymes and repetitious poems encourage the children to develop their auditory and manipulative skills. All this, done in an environment of fun and cosiness, is often repeated every week and is a crucial opportunity for the very young to develop their skills.

This is also a vital experience for parents (occasionally known for driving the storytime organizer mad by having a chat in the back row!) as they watch and listen, seeing the enjoyment of sharing, in their children's faces. Parents learn how to tell and read stories with excitement and often repeat these skills, learnt surreptitiously in the library, on a daily basis at home.

Those staff who are able to master the art of story-telling can take the experience onto a higher plane. Liz Weir, a veritable master of the craft, has written a booklet, *Boom cicer boom*,[4] which is highly recommended to all would-be story-tellers. Give it a go!

It is very easy to fall into the trap that every library must provide a storytime to a set formula every week, regardless of how many children attend. There should be clear criteria for the success of a session, related to how many children attend over three or four weeks, and an assessment should be made of the impact in relation to the cost of that session.

Can you put a price on literacy? No, but you do need to be prompted to ask questions about the effectiveness of all storytimes. If a storytime is held because it is the 'done thing' then its impact on the child will never be properly considered. It is likely to have little impact in any case if professionals have not thought through their reasons for doing it.

It may be that the audience suddenly starts to decline over a regular number of weeks. Why? Is it because regular attendees have started school? Or could it be because the ballet school has organized a new session for three-year-olds at the same time? Or perhaps the local school has changed its end-of-day time, which means that parents have to take their toddlers with them to pick up their older children from school, so cannot come to storytime. All these problems can be addressed if you know about them.

Some libraries have developed an imaginative programme of storytimes which build up over a number of weeks. To hold the imagination of toddlers and their carers, storytimes have been extended and a book-related activity added. This activity develops gradually, partly because toddlers cannot concentrate for very long and are quite slow at art and craft work. If, however, they can create a picture or model based on their story which develops week by week, they often get heavily involved and want to attend subsequent weeks.

Alternatively, in areas where there are already a great many events for young children, it may be better to hold a bigger event every month. Organized around a theme, stories and games can involve children for up to a couple of hours. The impact of the very regular weekly storytime is, of course, lost, but more time is available for children to interrelate, communicate, tell their stories and develop social skills and dexterity.

Whatever the approach, storytime offers huge learning opportunities that extend beyond the session. Some excellent work is taking place within some authorities where staff address the issue of how parents or carers can extend the impact of storytime between sessions. This works particularly well where storytime has been organized around a theme. Simple maths, language and science can be learned by simply building on a theme. For example, one storytime on the theme of feet included an activity organized around shoes and sole rubbings. This led to family sole rubbings and then on to playgroups where simple sets were introduced. Discussion of textures, bark rubbing and simple science followed. Debate about a few ideas at the end of each storytime can offer parents and carers ideas and make them feel very involved.

Holiday activities also are a vital part of literacy development. In many authorities activities have developed from 'stick and paste' which took a great deal of preparation, to exciting book-related activities such as story trails, book quizzes and reading challenges. Public libraries play an important, but little recognized, role in maintaining and often improving reading levels throughout the holidays. Many children who find reading boring, or a chore, suddenly blossom when it is taken out of the school environment and made fun. Many authorities tell of receiving grateful letters from parents relating their child's sudden-found reading confidence. Schools also tell of evidence of reading maintenance or improvement. Libraries should formalize this more, working with local schools to check reading ages of pupils before the holiday, re-checking them when they return and then assessing the difference. Cooperating with schools in this way can help to identify children with particular reading difficulties, and working with these children during the holidays can help them to crack the problem by getting into the reading habit.

Reading challenges take place in many authorities. There are differences of approach but most have the same aim: to make reading a fun, achievable goal that everyone can try. The importance of such an activity is that it is not a competition between children but a challenge to the individual. There may be friendly rivalry between peers, but this can be avoided if wished. Each child keeps a record of their reading in a log and comment on what they thought of each book. Children are encouraged to read widely and to try new authors or titles they do not know. Sometimes they are told to choose books from a list but the activity is just as successful if they are allowed to choose any book from the library. All the staff have to do is to check that children are not consistently reading books at too easy a level, and that they are completing their reviews.

Determining the reading ability of a child is difficult, and it should be remembered that children are on holiday and should not be continually forced to read books which stretch them. Why should adults be able to take blockbusters and escapist reading on holiday if children are not to be allowed to?

The reading challenge can be fitted around the holiday theme if there is one. The aim is to read to different levels. Each level is rewarded by a small prize, for example a badge. When a child reaches the target number of books, say 15, s/he is given a certificate. Some children will be capable of reading around the programme two or three times, others seven or eight, while others will manage to read just one stage. For all, however, it is a great achievement. It can be especially successful if arrangements can be made to present the certificates at school assembly or with a special celebration in the library.

Many authorities have held exciting reading challenges, for example Norfolk, Devon, Bedfordshire and Westminster, often with interesting sponsorship support. The benefits of this type of activity for the child and for the library service are:

For the children:
- it is fun
- they have something to aim for throughout the holiday
- children of all abilities can be involved: the books have to be right for them individually, not just taken from a specific area of the library
- children are challenging themselves to succeed
- there is no stigma of success or failure: everyone who reads one book or more succeeds
- they maintain their reading ability at or above their level, giving them a flying start in the new term
- many parents will tell you that the challenge made their child interested in reading.

For the library:
- it does not take much to organize
- it can be easily linked to a theme, often giving that theme added weight
- it has a huge impact on the library's issue figures
- it ensures a healthy turnover of stock
- staff are not tied to listening to large numbers of children talk about books because they write their reviews in a log book. General discussion with children every so often is all that is required.
- all staff can get involved and this builds confidence in working with children
- it can attract sponsorship.

Events, author visits and book-related activities are also continually contributing to the literacy development of children. Whether it is a person who brings snakes to meet the children, an author talking about their work or a theatre group, the interaction with the child is the same. They are developing listening and observation skills, they are learning to handle information and they are improving social skills.

Children's services attract a wide audience for activities, but events are not limited to within the library. Children's librarians often have excellent contacts with playschemes, refuges and special needs groups, and tailor-made activities are often organized for individual groups as a bridge to encourage their children to take part in events within the library.

Stock

The selection and arrangement of stock is a key component in the library's contribution to literacy development. Fun, attractive libraries with an inviting, cosy atmosphere are crucial to making children feel at home. Combining the needs of babies and toddlers with the growing sophistication of upper junior school children through to the often anarchic demands of teenagers is not easy, especially in a small space. Creating a space that does not interfere with the needs of other users of the rest of the library is even more complex.

The library has to be made up of a series of definable areas with clear progression between, but also providing the ability to dip back and forth between areas as children develop. Children with difficulties in reading should not have to feel humiliated in their search for easy reads; children with an advanced reading standard should be able to find material which challenges their reading abilities but does not exceed their emotional maturity. Clear guiding is essential, and the use of pictures as well as words is important. Children need to feel that this area is their space and that they are safe. They will usually ask for help if needed, but few libraries can staff the children's library full time, so it has to be easy for a child to find her/his way around. Guiding is something that children are now used to from their experience of shopping in supermarkets. The reading of signs is an important skill for adult life.

Book clubs, family reading groups and teenage reading clubs

These are all strands in the library's contribution to literacy. The involvement of parents, grandparents, carers, brothers and sisters or guardians in talking with children about books they have read can have phenomenal impact. Both adults and children gain much from the experience. To hear a parent or grandparent tell a group that on finding out how much a child enjoyed a book they themselves took it, read it and found it fascinating has a great impact on the members of the group. It is understandable for those who missed Tolkien, Susan Cooper or Peter Dickinson as children and are discovering them later in life, but when the discovery involves Anne Fine, Judith Kerr or Alan Ahlberg, the reader's strength of feeling makes a real impact on the group.

Much depends upon parents' willingness to get involved in groups like this. Often they start with their children in the junior years and continue right through to the teenage years. The groups are not limited to middle class, articulate parents and children, but can be made up of a cross-section of the local community. Much depends upon the effort put in to set them up. The aim is to encourage children to read for enjoyment as an alternative leisure activity. Reading groups provide parents with the opportunity to spend time choosing books with their children and to become aware of the wide range of titles which are now available. They maximize the opportunity for contact between librarians, children and parents and they remind parents and carers of the services of the library, reintroducing them to the borrowing and reading habit.

Children are encouraged to borrow freely from the fiction collection, either from the full range of stock or from a pre-selected collection chosen for their appeal and accessibility to a particular age group. For the first 20 minutes of the meeting parents and children return their books from the last session, browse, chat, have a drink and decide which book to talk about. After a while everyone settles down and the books are introduced. Children will make the most of book introductions themselves; however, adult involvement is also encouraged, with library staff, parents and carers joining in. The library staff role is often to introduce books which are new or different from the group norm, so ensuring that the reading of the group is constantly being challenged.

The outcomes of the reading group depend upon the children. As a result, children will view reading as a positive social activity and not something that you 'don't admit to'. Parents will learn about a wide range of books and do not have to resort to encouraging children to read very old favourites because they know nothing else. There is a marked increase in the children's confidence in their own ability to choose material and to discuss it. Dina Thorpe's *Reading for fun*[5] provides further information about this aspect of library groups. In addition, the library gains a higher profile in the locality. There are often stronger links between the school and the library staff. The feedback from readers to library staff assists in stock selection development, ensuring a more directed use of the budget.

Teenage reading clubs must be different in character. Parents are not encouraged to attend. The discussion these groups promote on books, general reading issues and social issues can play an important role in the lives and development of young people. Reading groups tend to attract teenagers and the discussions can often be intense. They also offer opportunities to discuss many other issues which concern teenagers, whether they be political issues or personal ones.

The benefits of both children's and teenage groups, for those taking part, are that the young readers are deeply involved in something that interests them. They talk and listen, they have to be able to summarize what they have read and, more importantly, what they think about it. It is one of the few opportunities for children to feel more important than adults and to be in the position of leader or even teacher. As far as the library is concerned, these sessions increase issues and turnover, staff become more familiar with stock, the library plays an important role and focal point in the community, and the value of these occasions in the development of reading for pleasure is underlined. If the general stock and the normal issue system are used, even with special cards, there is a minimum of preparation, especially if the children's librarian knows the stock well. This is also is an ideal opportunity for other members of staff to get involved and to develop their skills of talking to others and sharing their views on books.

Bookmarks, booklists, promotional displays

Children, like other readers, often need help in finding books that they might enjoy. The pressure on children to read is enormous, as parents and carers know that the skill is so vital throughout life. Parents of toddlers refuse to take wordless picture books just because they have no words, missing the point that visual literacy is just as vital a skill.

Stimulating displays are not the preserve of the artistic. The covers of children's books are attractive in themselves, and, with the number of posters available from publishers or suppliers, a display is quick, easy and valuable in bringing new books to the attention of children and their carers.

Booklists and bookmarks both for children and carers are also valuable. These can be centred around particular themes or aimed at particular readers. Parents often seek books to help children at the very beginning of their reading lives, and to stimulate the seven or eight-year-old who is not interested in books. Children, meanwhile, are frequently interested in horror stories, funny stories or adventure stories.

General promotion of stock

The key to assisting the development of children's reading is having a broad knowledge of the books in the library and talking to children about what they have read and enjoyed. Children do like a sense of adventure too and some really exciting book promotions can be developed at little cost. Rachel van Riel[6] has done a lot of work in exploding the myth that you have to be creative or artistic to promote books. Working with a wide range of library staff, she has tapped into a multitude of thoughts and ideas and shown how promotions can work, whatever your budget or library size.

There are many good promotional ideas within the profession which are and should be shared. One example is the 'surprise borrow', where a child borrows four books of her/his choice plus one wrapped in brown paper – a surprise! This is more difficult to organize than for adults because the reading ages need to match, but it can have great results. Organizing a competition to design a T-shirt of children's favourite books and then getting the winning one printed is a fun way to organize a review scheme. If you ask the children to design their covers on A4 size cut-out paper T-shirts, and then hang them on a washing line through, across or around your library, not only do you have a fun competition but other children want to read some of the books that the T-shirts have been designed around.

Getting the children to write to famous people to find out their favourite children's book has many benefits. The children have to develop their writing and communication skills and, once the replies come in, their reviewing and critical skills develop as they assess what they think of the choice.

There are many more brilliant ideas which can be used to help children develop reading skills in a fun environment. Apart from the usual activities that a library would expect to provide to contribute to literacy development, certain initiatives exist which are specifically designed to improve literacy standards:

Bookstart

This is an idea which originated in the USA, was trialed in Birmingham and is now being introduced by a number of authorities under a range of names. The concept is straightforward: to provide every baby at their eight-month health check with a book or library pack. The eight-month check was chosen partly because every baby has to have one, and partly because at that stage parents are beginning to think about their child's development. It is also a good time to introduce a child to books as they are beginning to focus on things and to listen to the sound of a soothing voice.

It is beneficial that the pack is distributed at the health check rather than in a library environment. This means that all parents and carers will receive a pack and be encouraged to use the library rather than just those who already visit it. The pack usually contains a book, a poster, bookmark or sticker details about the local library, story-telling times and a membership card. Materials are written in the language most appropriate to the family concerned.

All authorities who run the scheme have reported that it makes a huge impact. There has been an increase in library membership of both children and adults. Many parents or carers have reported that the pack is the first thing a child has owned, and for some it has opened up opportunities never before thought of as being available for both children and adults. There is currently research under way to assess whether the scheme is having any long-term effects on the reading levels of children. Early reports from this and other research abroad suggest that children introduced to books at a very early stage will begin reading sooner and have a wider grasp of vocabulary. Researchers are following the progress of children involved in the Birmingham project through to the end of their first year at school to assess the impact of the initiative.

The potential impact of such schemes as Bookstart on lifelong reading is reinforced in many reports, the most recent of which is *Heavy book borrowers*.[8] This report investigates the habits of 'heavy borrowers'. One of the main findings is that such individuals mostly became enthusiastic about reading when they were young.

Reading events

Working with others in the local community can also help to initiate reading events. Education 2000 has been responsible for developing a 'Read It' a campaign in some of its areas. This is a community-wide literacy campaign which has captured the energy and enthusiasm of many in the community, including the business sector. The campaign has two objectives. Firstly, it aims to raise awareness across the community of the importance of literacy by offering opportunities for children to become involved and to become members of 'Read It'. Secondly, 'Read It' sites are to be developed which aim to sustain community-based reading.

Libraries in Leeds, for example, have become heavily involved in the scheme, along with schools, community centres and religious organizations. 'Read It' packs include reading games and activities appropriate to the children's age, writing materials and information about libraries to encourage their use. Members regularly send in their reading cards and completed activity books. In Leeds book loans have gone up as a result, and children are joining the library in order to be able to keep on reading.

Reading is Fundamental UK[9]

RIF is an organization that was set up to help children grow up to love books and reading. It has five aims:

- to provide books for children to choose and own at no cost to them or their families
- to show children that reading can be fun
- to help parents to become involved with their children's reading
- to help families enjoy stories and books together
- to create new generations of readers.

The initiative is supported by Tate and Lyle, and is based at the National Literacy Trust. RIF in the United States has resulted in:

- reading test scores improving
- children spending more time reading
- children being more positive towards reading and more eager to learn
- more books being borrowed from the library
- parents encouraging more reading at home
- the community as a whole getting involved.

Much more than books

Most libraries have collections of talking books and book-related videos which also contribute to the development of literacy skills. Talking books are a way of bringing books alive for children with reading or visual difficulties; they are also good for use in the car, or for those who want to read something that is beyond their current skill level. There is a wide range of excellently read tapes to listen to. Libraries tend not to have enough of these, either because they are too expensive or because they are poorly packaged. We urgently need all suppliers to follow the lead of Askews' 'Sound Promising' in tackling this issue, as cassettes need to be imaginatively packaged to promote use by looking attractive on the library shelf.

Libraries need to cooperate in circulating stock, so keeping collections of talking books interesting and inviting but keeping their cost level reasonable. The same can be said for videos. Again, these are valuable for children with reading difficulties or hearing problems. Some authorities do not provide videos in all of their libraries, and some avoid children's videos altogether. This is because of concern that parents may just sit their child down in front of a video rather than of interacting with the child, sharing and discussing what is being watched.

Videos bring life to a story or a situation and can develop auditory and observation skills. The library should choose the best available. There is some awful video material available, particularly under the guise of early learning materials on number, colour, alphabet, etc. A number of authorities do not allow children to borrow videos on their own ticket because of concern about classification for different age groups. Clear signs reminding users of the certification scheme, and exactly who can borrow what, should be clearly displayed. Authorities which do encourage children to use their own ticket normally either train counter staff to be vigilant, or have developed automated systems to trigger potential problems.

Computer software, particularly CD-ROM, is now widely available from the interactive picture book to some stunning interactive information texts. Many children are excited by computers, and particularly by the interactive nature of the best CD-ROMs. Again, it is easy to get carried away with the technology, but there is a great deal of poor material available. Material must be interactive, and it must add another dimension to a book. If all you are getting for your money is a straight reproduction of a book, there is very little point in investing in the CD-ROM format.

A reasonable degree of literacy is required to use many CD-ROMs in order to make them work or to follow the on-screen instructions. They continually stretch the vocabulary and the reading skills simply by following the programme. At whichever level, the interactive story or the higher level text, they are extremely useful for children with poor manipulative or verbal skills. When there is no need for them to write, but simply to manipulate a large mouse, these children are enabled to work from the same base as their contemporaries, and will be able to move around the screen easily in order to find out what they want to know. All PC-based software and superhighway access demands and develops literacy.

There is some concern amongst teachers that the literacy demands of the Internet are too high for many children. Watching children of whatever ability using the Internet is fascinating: they need time and some help to navigate to the correct site, but their questioning of the screen and of each other is a revelation, and they far surpass their 'normal' reading level. Children need a range of skills to use the Internet, including selecting the required source of information, skimming, scanning, picture interpretation skills, use of indexes and search engines, the ability to question the absence of information and development of a language of classification.

The NCET project on evaluating CD-ROM titles[10] also found that CD-ROMs encourage children to use books more rather than less. This is reflected in public library use. Children seem well able to integrate their work on the computer with research from books. It does not take long for the novelty of computers to wear off, and the software to be seen as just another tool to gain information. Children's use of books, on the contrary, becomes more critical, and they begin to question them, and to find their way around the layout and the information much better.

An equally fascinating discovery is that using a computer, whether for CD-ROM or for the Internet, can develop the social skills of those children who find it difficult to relate to other children. Two children who do not normally communicate well can work happily together in front of a screen – an added bonus in developmental terms.

Family literacy

Family literacy programmes target both parents and their children, and can reduce failure rate as well as help parents improve their basic skills. Family literacy is not the answer to all the problems of low attainment: however, it is a major contribution to preventing failure. Since 1993 the National Foundation for Educational Research (NFER) has been funding four intensive family literacy demonstration programmes. They aim to improve:

• the literacy skills of parents
• parents' ability to help their children with the early stages of learning to read and write
• young children's acquisition of reading and writing.

The study found that children made greater than expected improvements in vocabulary and reading, that substantial improvements were made in writing and that there were substantial increases in literacy-related home activities. For parents, their own reading levels improved.

Family literacy is a successful way of raising the achievement levels of the whole family. It works to improve the skills everyone needs to get the most from education, and reaches children who might otherwise fail. It starts early in family life, when there is most impact and its effects will last. Libraries need to get involved as projects develop nationally, in partnership with organizations such as adult basic skills services, local education authorities, schools, colleges, and Training Enterprise Councils (TECs).

References

1   Mark, J., *Thunder and lightnings*, Harmondsworth, Puffin, 1976.
2   *The new generation: a report on attitudes and behaviour of primary school children*, Handel Communications,
3   The school is Litherland High School, Sefton, Merseyside. See *Managing Schools Today*, **4** (2), 1994/5, 18.
4   Weir, L., *Boom cicer boom*, Library Association Youth Libraries Group.
5   Thorpe, D, *Reading for fun*, Cranfield, Cranfield Press, 1988.
6   van Riel, R., Opening the book, Pontefract Road, Pontefract WF8 3NH.

7   Shelf Talk, *Promoting literature in public libraries*, The Arts Council of England and The Library Association.

8   *Heavy book borrowers: a report of the leisure habits of key library users*, Book Marketing Ltd, 1996.

9   Reading is Fundamental UK, National Literacy Trust, Swire House, 59 Buckingham Gate, London SW1E 6AJ.

10   National Council for Educational Technology, *Evaluating CD-ROM titles*, 1996. Available from NCET, Milburn Hill Road, Science Park, Coventry CV4 7AL along with other valuable publications.

8
Stock related issues

I often put books up there if they never get borrowed. *The Windmill Children*'s got an awful cover and no pictures, so no one wants it, but if it's up on the board someone might think it's good and take it home.

J. Mark, *The dead letter box*[1]

Stock is one of the fundamental building blocks of the children's service, impinging as it does on many aspects of service provision. All aspects of stock should be looked at as a whole and managed globally. If not, the service will be incapable of reaching its full potential. This approach is referred to as 'total collection management' and requires work to be done on:

- community profiles, to understand the needs and wants of the locality
- stock profiles, to assess what is required in which section and why
- budget allocation
- stock selection
- stock arrangement and editing
- promotion
- performance and auditing.

This is an iterative process, and each stage needs to inform the next. One of the key facets of total collection management is a set of clear guidelines or principles.

Stock guidelines or policy

The assessment and selection of books and other materials is of fundamental importance in children's libraries. It is important therefore that the key principles appropriate for an authority are drawn together in a policy statement or set of guidelines.

Any selection guidelines or principles should be intended as a source document for all librarians and their staff. They should provide practical guidance on all aspects of selection and editing in relation to work with young people. All selection and editing in individual libraries should be seen in the wider context of the authority. Community librarians and children's librarians should work in liaison and, where such posts exist, with their young people's service specialists.

Guidelines will vary from authority to authority, and will concentrate on different issues to reflect priorities in relation to their users' needs. They will also need to be written in a style appropriate to that authority. Below are some broad principles or examples which could be used as a basis for the development of stock selection guidelines.

The purpose of stock

All libraries should provide a selection of attractive and easily available material, which should:

- help children in the expansion of knowledge
- help children come to terms with new experiences and extend their imagination
- encourage children to read for enjoyment
- help children to understand their own and other people's situations
- develop a child's emotional and intellectual growth
- cultivate and extend a child's use and understanding of language
- further children's awareness and understanding of their own and other cultural groups
- help all children develop a love of books.

Leicestershire Library and Information Service summarize provision in the following way:

- to provide pleasure and enjoyment through identifying and responding to genuine child demand
- to develop and maintain enthusiasm for reading amongst children who are learning to read, becoming readers and becoming learners
- to develop and maintain children and young people's use and understanding of language, and through this their confidence in their own skills and abilities
- to meet children's information needs, stimulate enquiry and foster the development of both critical awareness and information skills

- to help children to self-knowledge and to respect their own cultural heritage and that of different ethnic and cultural groups
- to offer a balanced view of our own society and that of the wide world, contributing positive images and reflecting the County Council's equal opportunities policy
- to prepare and assist the pleasure of choice as well as being proactive in making a choice
- to afford children the pleasure of shared experience between child and adult, especially child and parent.

Stock in libraries should continue to support the young person in all the above points as they come to terms with the adult world through:

- self-discovery
- the wider world of leisure and work
- life and social skills
- formal and continuing education.

Use of children's services should be extended to adults caring for children, and this will have implications on stock selection. The provision of relevant books and information will contribute to:

- knowledge of child development (e.g. health and welfare, education, hobbies and activities)
- an awareness of how children cope with new experiences
- an understanding of how a child acquires the skills of listening, talking, reading and writing
- adults' ability to support children in their educational and life growth.

Stock provision
Local needs must be taken into account when planning a stock provision policy. Contact with, and knowledge and awareness of, local organizations and groups in the community is of paramount importance. The drawing up of a community profile can be vital in planning stock provision, for example, types of schools, predominant age groups, languages and the range of cultural groups in the area. When approached from the users' perspective, the key considerations become clear. Stock should:

- balance user requirements with the need to reflect and promote the needs of our multicultural society
- provide for all levels of ability from the less able child to the gifted child, and for varying levels of interest, including parents and casual users
- provide an exciting range of experiences for those with special needs
- meet the needs of all ages from the very youngest to the person who is ready to use the adult library
- cover relevant areas in fiction and non-fiction with both book and non-book material
- provide books and other material to stimulate leisure reading (e.g. games, jokes, quizzes, pet-keeping, dinosaurs).

Issues to consider in planning a stock provision policy

Taking this approach raises a number of questions or issues which a good policy needs to address. Answers to the following questions as presented within the policy will ensure a comprehensive approach:

- What are the strengths and weaknesses of existing stock?
- What is the balance between maintaining a stock of the best available titles which have proved useful and popular, and the importance of purchasing newly-published material?
- Should a saturation policy for notable and popular children's books be developed?
- What is the role of paperbacks, and are they to be bought for all sections or just for some?
- Should stock reflect the National Curriculum in total or in part?
- Should there be as wide a range of stock on the shelves as possible to enable librarians to respond immediately to children's interests, or is it better not to aim for a totally comprehensive subject coverage, concentrating on areas more in demand?
- What should the level of provision be in different sections of stock? Older fiction and non-fiction is often over-represented, and insufficient space is devoted to materials for younger children. Do not neglect aspects of materials in popular demand such as songs, riddles, jokes, popular poetry, collecting and hobbies
- Stock provision will include not only book and non-book material but pamphlets, ephemera, information sources and periodicals. Special

consideration may have to be given to these areas to boost provision.
- What is the role and provision of IT? Is it seen as a format and included in all the above or are there special IT stock guidelines?

Arrangement

However good the acquisition of stock, it will largely remain static unless complemented by thoughtful arrangement and promotion. The following are some of the issues which need to be thought through:

- The needs of the user should take precedence over the convenience of the library staff and therefore careful thought should be given to the sequence of shelving and arrangement of stock.
- Stock should be arranged using the authority-agreed categories. A process to ensure that all libraries within one authority have classified the same book in the same category may be considered – or this may be seen as too rigid.
- Special collections can play an important role. These can be fun books, quick reads, picture books for older children, parents' collections, etc.
- Displays can be a useful impetus to exploiting stock.
- Less formal arrangements such as play crates or 'designer' kinder boxes are ideal for attracting younger children.
- Books for younger children should be placed at a suitable height on safe shelving.
- Special consideration needs to be given, with adult library staff, to the needs of younger and older teenagers and the siting of appropriate collections. Some librarians have found valuable a 15+ section in the adult library and, where space permits, 'bridging' collections are useful. Consideration should also be given to non-fiction and information material in teenage collections. This topic is addressed in the section on strategy for services to young people (page 98).

Guiding

Having tackled acquisition and arrangement of stock, how children and young people find what they are looking for is the next fundamental issue. Clear, simple guiding will help all users to access the resources effectively. Points to consider are:

- A simple plan of the overall arrangement of the library is always helpful.
- Clear and simple guiding suitable for use by children is essential in all libraries: bay and block guiding must keep up to date as stock expands or contracts.
- Labels bearing the class number should be clear with faded and missing labels replaced immediately.
- Wherever possible, oversize books should not be shelved separately but if they are, then guiding should indicate this fact.

Display and promotion

Display

In considering displays and promotion, it is important not only to look at the children's section, but to consider displays within the adult library and in the wider community:

- For children, the cover of a book is an important incentive. It is recommended that face-forward displays are used throughout the whole age range. Unreachable higher shelving can be adapted for this purpose.
- Regular changing of displays can overcome the inadequacies of stock in smaller libraries/mobiles/trailers, by highlighting examples of other resources, e.g.:
  - talking books
  - teenage materials
  - language materials.
- Posters, friezes, mobiles and attractive furnishings will greatly enhance the environment of a children's reading area and can often be acquired free from library suppliers or local shops.
- Regularly changing small displays will be most effective in increasing awareness of particular books and authors.
- New booklists present an opportunity for creating displays.

Promotion

When looking at promotion all opportunities should be sought. For example:

- Opportunity should be taken to offer information about local museums, clubs, societies and leisure activities and to link into local events.

- Promotion should be organized to link with televised children's books, Carnegie and Greenaway and other medal winners, topical issues, information for parents.
- Excellent promotional opportunities can be made using children's own work, either on particular themes or authors, or on their favourite books.
- Finally, an excellent idea, where space permits, is to encourage children to come in and display their own activities on noticeboards throughout the library.

Funding

An authority's guidelines would need to indicate the bookfund allocation and how it is spent. This often means replicating part of the budget strategy identifying the necessary percentages. When new developments in education such as parenting, National Vocational Qualifications (NVQs), GCSE and National Curriculum, are likely to have particular impact upon the stock, initial separate funding should be sought to cover these areas. When looking at the funding principles of the stock, the following issues need to be addressed:

- It is necessary to examine individual patterns of use, size of library and nature of the community before determining shelf stock in specific areas of use, but it should be remembered that issues for younger material and picture books are very high and a good replacement policy needs to be maintained.
- Too much of the materials fund should not be spent on lower issue material to the detriment of potential high issue material.
- At the same time, a policy to support new authors should be considered.
- The proportion of stock on the shelves should be clearly indicated for all libraries and should relate to the specification of the service and measures identified. One example (not a recommendation) is:
  - Information books   25%
  - Picture books and younger readers   between 35% and 40%
  - Older children and paperbacks   approximately 35%.
- A proportion of the allocation in each category should be spent on

'fun' books, to stimulate sheer enjoyment in using books and libraries.
- It is suggested that a significant proportion of individual allocations should be spent on the replacement of well-established and popular items.

Selection

Selection of stock is very important, and a clear strategy is required. Stock is very valuable and there is a wide range of publishers. With such a huge number of new titles being published each year it is important that scarce resources are used prudently:

- There is no substitute for personal reading and knowledge of children's books. Both wide reading and specialist and individual interests are valued, and contribute to the shared expertise within an authority.
- Valid contributions to selection and reviewing can also be made by children, teachers, parents, colleagues and others interested in using and reading children's books.
- Stock selection should be constantly kept under review. Librarians should be aware of needs in contemporary society, and should be sensitive to the needs of special groups.
- A range of appropriate non-book materials is an essential addition to stock.

Issues to consider in book selection

Use a balanced judgment and historical perspective when looking at books published in less aware times, when social mores were different – especially when these have intrinsic literary value. Material published for the first time should be stringently examined and staff should select:

- for the reader: remember not only existing readers but potential library users and those with special needs.
- for the wider community: we all live in a multicultural society.
- material which portrays people of all cultures and both sexes in a positive way. Avoid material which denigrates particular sections of society or work, or is overtly or covertly sexist or racist.
- publications which have an imaginative and creative quality thus achieving a true or striking portrayal. Avoid items that are didactic or propagandist.

- so as not to avoid controversial or ethically, socially or politically sensitive issues, but to ensure that the stock selected presents well-reasoned and well-written choices or contributes to the debate.
- for the children's library in relation to adult and teenage stock. Children's material may be equally suitable for adult needs or vice versa. Some duplication may be valid in this context.
- to match user groups and specific user needs as closely as possible by the provision of appropriate materials at the right level of presentation.
- stock irrespective of format if it meets user needs. Difficulties of housekeeping and storage can be overcome to provide a good range of non-standard items, e.g. board books, pop-up books, CD-ROMs, non-standard paperbacks, oversized books, videos, pamphlets and ephemera, floor books.
- using the same criteria for retrospective purchase for purposes of stock editing as that adopted for the assessment and review of newly published material.
- using retrospective booklists issued by The Library Association Youth Libraries Group, Books for Keeps, Signal and other organizations and authorities.

Issues to consider when selecting CD-ROMs

CD-ROMs are quite expensive in relation to the price of books and it is vital to check that they offer value for money. CD-ROMs often combine audio, text, video clips and animation and those with huge resource banks require well-developed information skills to retrieve the information. It is easy to be attracted by the graphics and the action sequences, but careful assessment is required to get the best out of the material, and to match it to the needs of users and to gaps in information provision.

The content and the technical aspects of a disc need to be evaluated, and a common set of questions established, such as the commonsense 'Will it run on our machines?' The National Council for Educational Technology's (NCET) valuable guide *Evaluating CD-ROM titles*,[2] is designed for schools, but the issues are much the same. Their suggested questions to ask are reproduced here by kind permission, but the whole leaflet is recommended as it adds valuable detail:

Content and coverage
- How appropriate is the quantity of information?
- Does it fit well with the curriculum?
- What is the source of the information?
- Is it biased culturally or nationally?
- What is its cultural and moral tone?
- What is the balance of text, illustrations, audio and video?

Currency and accuracy
- When was it published?
- Is this the most recent version?
- How accurate is the information?
- Does it contain facts or just opinions?

National Curriculum
- Which subjects/topics does it cover?
- Which key stage does it address?

Reading age
- Is the vocabulary, structure and sentence length suitable?
- Does it have a built-in dictionary or glossary?
- Are differentiated versions of the text available?
- Does the retrieval of information depend heavily on correct spelling?
- Is there an audio option?

User interface
- Are the buttons, menus and icons clear?
- Is it obvious how the information is organized?
- Is on-screen help available?

Indexing and navigation
- Is navigation easy?
- Are there alternative routes through the material?
- How easy is it to retrieve information?
- Is there an index?
- Is there a contents menu?
- Presentation: what is the quality of illustrations?
- Can the audio and video elements be controlled?
- Can you alter colours and size of text?

Facilities and features
- Can you print and save selected material?
- Can you record what users have seen?
- Can information be tagged and marked?

For public libraries the leisure use and interests of children would need to be added.

Owing to the cost of CD-ROMs, schools are buying materials specifically to support the National Curriculum, although some are buying talking story books designed for the home market. This can mean that a topic like 'Dinosaurs', which would be a popular disc with children, is not available in many schools because it is not part of the curriculum. Public libraries have an important role to play in providing this sought-after material.

The NCET (SCET in Scotland) are a valuable source of information on CD-ROMs and all things IT. They understand the role of both school and public libraries, and often recommend their use to schools. They produce a comprehensive catalogue of children's CD-ROMs with excellent reviews entitled *CD-ROM in education: CD-ROM titles review*. Whilst written from the school's point of view, it is still appropriate. NCET also produce valuable leaflets for parents on such topics as home computers, children and video games, learning together using a computer, and the development of information skills.

Graphic novels
Graphic novels are a relatively new category in libraries. These are books for adults and teenagers, and they are valuable in the library context because they attract high issues, they appeal to 'non-users', they are relatively cheap and they make good display material. They maintain the interest of users who might otherwise drift away from libraries, and they can be used as the basis of excellent creative activity sessions for young people, by getting them to create their own storyboard version of their favourite book.

When selecting stock of graphic novels, most of the usual issues apply. It is necessary to check the author/artist, the subject matter, the content and its intended audience, the publisher and, finally, the production standard. Essential reading to find out more about graphic novels are the Youth Libraries Group's *Graphic account*[3] and *Books with attitude*.[4]

Assessment and reviewing

Many authorities run a scheme for the assessment and reviewing of books, computer software and audiovisual materials for children's libraries, which forms the basis of selection. In addition to this scheme, there will be a need to keep abreast of a balanced selection of professional journals and reviews. Librarians bear a responsibility for liaison with the book trade on such matters as the availability of books, and should act as a channel for communication on the appropriateness of material, on readers' needs not currently being met and on the accuracy of materials.

There has been a major change in the way authorities select books as a result of the demise of the Net Book Agreement. Approvals collections kept by many authorities, often in multiple sets, now attract a premium when negotiating tenders with suppliers because they are not a cost-effective process for the supplier. While no supplier has yet refused to provide approvals, both they and some authorities are looking for alternative approaches.

CD-ROM approvals

To avoid the expense of approval sets, a number of suppliers, including those specializing in children's materials, have invested in the development of CD-ROMs which list all new publications. Many are limited to books and audio tapes. Most provide good reproductions of the front cover and an inside spread, providing bibliographic details and order facilities. This method has the advantage of ease of use and, being on computer, provides the additional bonus of totalling the order and acting as an order record, thus reducing the workload at the library end. The best systems also contain book reviews, thus meeting some of the higher level requirements of some authorities.

With electronic data interchange (EDI) links, some CD-ROMs also can be linked into the authority's order system, providing cataloguing and order files for the authority as well. Currently the telecom specification for most authorities does not allow the maximum use of these CD-ROMs, as the network capabilities are limited by the slow telecom structure. Soon, however, the technology will catch up to allow networking between libraries at relatively low cost.

CD-ROM, however, is possibly only an intermediate or transient technology. The development of the information superhighway will allow purchasing over the Internet, using a very similar system to CD-

ROM but one which is quicker and more up to date. A choice of either collections by theme or a listing of all new books can be placed on the Net, as will eventually a complete list of suppliers', or even publishers', stock. One supplier at least is trialing this technology. Within a few years it will have developed further, and the system may even be secure enough to allow the children themselves to select a proportion of the stock using the new technology.

Owing to the innovative nature of the latest developments in technology, the profession is also having to cope with a major change in culture and, in fact, some may see this as actually attacking the very foundation of what being a children's librarian – or even providing a children's library service – is all about. Another view, however, is that it can revolutionize stock selection. In the past, too much time and cost has been invested in getting a book, tape, video or piece of software to the shelf that should or could be spent on exploiting the same item. It is vital to place the best and most appropriate material on the shelves. If this can be done more quickly, more easily and to the same level of quality by others doing the work, then we should consider letting go of the task. We can then maximize the potential of what we are also good at – promotion of the material to develop literacy and general skills. Staff will be able to concentrate on reading and exploiting what has already been bought, rather than having to read a huge raft of material only to purchase a very small percentage.

Book purchase

A balanced approach which utilizes a mix of new book buying processes: visits to suppliers' showrooms, purchase from nominated local bookshops, catalogues, lists and printouts, will be necessary. Often joint book-buying with the schools library service staff can be mutually beneficial where relevant. It is important not to overlook the use of non-standard suppliers and organizations, such as community publications, children's own writing, specialist overseas bookshops, and local and national organizations.

Editing and maintenance

Stock

A great deal of attention is paid to selecting stock but if equal consideration is not made of it once it is on the shelves then a total approach to stock will not be maintained. It is important to look at the stock in general – its physical condition in particular. The following are valuable points to consider:

- Stock editing is essential to achieve a balanced, informed, interesting and current stock, and the process should be a continuous one.
- The method of maintenance employed can vary, e.g. one category of stock may be dealt with at one particular time: picture books, younger readers, paperbacks or a non-fiction subject area.
- A regular check is necessary to ensure that all out-dated editions of popular or useful materials are replaced.
- Continued familiarity with stock will reveal its strengths and weaknesses, especially gaps in subject coverage, and should result in a sound economic purchasing policy.

Physical condition
It is important to check that stock is in good condition in order to ensure its durability. The following procedure is recommended:

- Damaged or mistreated items should be removed in order to ensure attractive stock.
- Non-book media should be scrutinized with the same care and attention, and damaged material either replaced or repaired.
- Is the book in good condition internally? Picture book covers have a habit of lasting longer than the inside.

Stock performance management
Local editing and stock maintenance should be supported by an annual stock edit and use of annual management data as described in Part 1. This ensures the cyclical nature of stock management, guarantees that use informs selection and that personal bias cannot influence a whole collection too strongly.

References
1   Mark, J., *The dead letter box*, Harmondsworth, Puffin, 1982.
2   National Council for Educational Technology, *Evaluating CD-ROM titles*, 1996. Available from NCET, Milburn Hill Road,

Science Park, Coventry CV4 7AL along with other valuable publications.

3   Barker, K. (ed.), *Graphic account: the selection and promotion of graphic novels in libraries for young people*, The Library Association Youth Libraries Group, 1993.

4   *Books with attitude*, booklist, Bishop and Barnicoat Library Suppliers, Cornwall, 1996.

9
Education

'I thought you didn't like learning things' said Andrew.
'That wasn't learning that was just finding out'.

J. Mark, *Thunder and lightnings*[1]

The changing approach to education

The face of education is changing. The needs of education, the role of
parents or carers, skills development and performance of individuals
and institutions are all under the spotlight. Developments in response to
these issues appear to be going in two completely different and incom-
patible directions. While this is unsettling it does create a breach into
which libraries must step. The key elements of these two conflicting
developments are the strong framework set by governments for the curriculum, and the increasing pressure for local learning within the community.

The curriculum and community learning

On the one hand governments throughout the world are placing a strong
grip on education, compartmentalizing learning, emphasizing individual achievement and overlaying a fairly inflexible curriculum with huge
resource demands. Libraries and the skills they demand are vital in this
arena, and at last information-handling skills are being recognized
throughout the curriculum. So is the need for extensive support material. Unfortunately, this is happening at the same time as a weakening or
even disintegration of schools library services through delegation of
budgets or savage cuts – or both – and through cuts in budgets of individual schools.

At the same time, the type of learning demanded by this curriculum
is not the only type of learning one needs for later life. This is being recognized by the current mounting pressure from organizations such as
Education 2000 for community learning and the creation of a learning
society. This exposes the need for collaborative learning, based on the

active support of the home and community and the technologies of information and communication. It stresses that the greatest weakness of the present curriculum is its failure to promote real understanding. Fundamental to this concept is the development of information handling skills and support resources. The difference is that this approach also recognizes that any expenditure on learning resources – books, videos or computers – is extremely productive.

While all children need both a body of knowledge and some basic skills to be functionally literate, our rapidly changing society demands that young people rise above this, to think critically and creatively, to be flexible and spontaneous. No longer are there jobs for life. New workers need to be 'empowered'. We need to encourage a new type of learning, creating the desire for knowledge and the ability to acquire it, the use of past experience to understand the present situation and then to formulate action for the future.

If libraries grasp this opportunity, the way forward could lead to a great future. We need to investigate the concept (highlighted by John Abbott in the UK at the ASCEL launch) that libraries should become the learning mode in the community. His work combines thinking from the USA and a number of European countries amongst others. As schools change their role, he sees secondary schools as having a limited future – or even none – and, instead learning taking place within the whole local community.

> Schooling in the future must involve both learning in school and learning through a variety of community experiences. Young people require a 'new learning environment', made up partly of formal schooling and partly of informal learning opportunities, so that they receive the support not only of teachers but of other adults.
>
> J. Abbott, *Learning makes sense*[2]

In reaction to this type of thinking the move to community schools is growing. Abbott's view is further developed by a British Library supported article by John Martyn, 'Twenty years on'.[3] He asserts that, because of increasing reliance on remote teaching and use of computer communication equipment in the education process, it will become harder for sectors of society that are unable to afford access to communication channels to break into the education system and to acquire an education. In his view it is conceivable that the public library could offer the only way out of this 'ghetto', thus returning to one of the original motives for its creation.

The direction in which education is moving is constantly shifting. It does, however, seem to be further and further towards an acceptance that it is the acquisition of information skills which is vital. The ability to find information, analyse it, gather arguments, hypothesize, weigh up the information, make judgments, solve problems, innovate, design, reflect, summarize and evaluate are crucial for the future. There have been numerous different ways of describing these skills and of defining the hierarchy of learning, but ultimately they can be summed up by The Library Association's leaflet *Curriculum guidance: National Curriculum and effective learning*,[4] which has taken the National Curriculum in the UK and identified six key issues in information handling. These are: planning; locating and gathering; selecting and appraising; organizing and recording; communicating and realizing; and, finally, evaluating. It demonstrates the relationship between these skills and the specific programmes of study, and will be a valuable asset for all types of work with children and young people.

Supporting learning

It is obvious from all this that the public library has the opportunity to play a major role in the education of children. Local libraries must work with the approach to schooling prevalent in their area. Many are a long way from realizing that learning takes place in the whole community and that the library has a clear role to play. Many schools in the UK have even reduced their visits to the library, partly owing to the implementation of the Children Act with its requirement for a greater number of supervisors accompanying children, and partly owing to the increased pressure on classroom time brought about by the demands of the UK National Curriculum.

Class visits

Changes in the nature of school visits to libraries offer an opportunity for library staff to examine and revitalize the class visit, and then re-market it. Westminster City Libraries have done just that, and have produced the following plan outlining the aims of a class visit programme:

• To promote the use of libraries by encouraging individual children to use the library outside school hours

- To increase contacts and links with schools
- To promote the enjoyment of reading and libraries
- To encourage lifelong learning via an information skills programme.

By analysing content, length of visit and frequency, the plan looks at what might be achieved in class visits of the future. In discussion with schools, it was decided to plan longer visits for Key Stage 2 pupils, with more emphasis on information handling skills, while the visits would stay the same for younger pupils.

For Key Stage 2 class visits Westminster City Libraries have produced packs based on various themes to use on class visits. Each theme has three elements: book material; oral telling; and library skills-based activities, including general library use, care of books, alphabetical skills, location skills, reference skills, and CD-ROM. Initial evaluation has shown that teachers value and appreciate the longer visits. Stockport Library Service has also produced an excellent class visit/information skills programme based around themed packs.

Where a wider view of education prevails in the area, the library must become involved in its development, or it will become sidelined. It must not be assumed that schools will come to the library. In many secondary schools where this educational view is developing it is the school library which is expanding and attempting to develop its role, sometimes to the detriment of the public library.

Recommendation One of *Investing in children*,[5] which encourages the development of an integrated strategy, becomes obvious and easy to understand in this context. In reality such a strategy is proving much harder to achieve. A number of authorities have produced a leaflet identifying what parents, teachers and governors can expect from the public and schools library services. For further information, see 'An integrated strategy' in Part 2 and 'Working together' in the next chapter.

Homework support

One of the most obvious ways a public library can support the work of local schools and become involved in the community approach to education is the development of homework support. As with literacy, for many services this will, to begin with at least, require repackaging and redevelopment of existing services.

Most libraries provide non-fiction resources, and these are the base for homework collections. The curriculum has resulted in pupils from the full range of local schools studying the same topic at the same time, which has aggravated the already severe difficulty of responding to project homework. This has been further complicated for some libraries by the devolution of the schools library service budget resulting in schools having to pay for their own services. This has further resulted in some teachers attempting to borrow all the available books on one subject on their family tickets, and then sending in their class to do their homework. Libraries do not stand a chance of responding to their real customer, the individual child, in this situation, and some children who found no support may not come back.

As a result, libraries are forced to put the most popular homework stock on short loan for a week, a day or for use in the library only. The best practice keeps this stock integrated with the rest of the non-fiction so that children do not have more than one place to look for books and they can browse through other material. Collections must stay fluid, and books should not stay permanently on short loan, but should follow the curriculum. Many may see this practice as restrictive, but it has impressive results.

The response from parents has been very positive. They feel reassured that their children will be able to find some material on their project, and are pleased that the short loan approach seems to have developed responsibility to get the work done so that the book can go back on time. They feel that the system is fair, and that every child has the chance to obtain some material, even including those who always leave their homework until the last minute. Homework support has also prevented teachers from stripping the library of key stock, thus forcing them to use the schools library services (where they exist) which have the appropriate resources to meet needs.

In addition, library staff feel much more satisfied that everyone has a chance to find material they need. They feel that information handling skills are developing more quickly, and that children have much more of a sense of purpose when they come in, as they have formulated their question and know what they want. Issues are going up, which for some libraries means additional bookfund or staffing. Before the advent of short loan collections staff had to deal with enquiries but, because of the number of books which had already been borrowed, they had no evidence of their effort.

Homework centres or clubs

Homework support is now being successfully extended into homework centres and clubs. There is strong support for such developments from government, the Prince's Trust and other agencies. Some schools are opening them, but libraries can often offer more access opportunities, being open longer hours.

There are many variations on the funding and organization of homework centres, which build on the library's basic stock provision together with IT resources and adult assistance with the enquiries. They often cover GCSE level support as well as junior and lower secondary school work. Their aim is to encourage life-long learning skills, to enhance educational achievement and to empower young people. The objectives are:

- to provide additional support and 'safe spaces' for young people after school
- to develop the education, skills and employment prospects of young people
- to tackle under-achievement in schools
- to tackle poverty by increasing access to information and information technology
- to promote equality of opportunity for all children
- to enhance the quality of life of local young people
- to overcome the problems of rural and urban deprivation by increasing opportunities for access to information
- to assist young people in developing information handling skills and the exploitation of all media forms
- to establish or confirm the library as a place for support.

David Murray in his excellent ASCEL briefing paper *Homework help clubs*[6] explains what homework help clubs do:

> Basically a homework help club operates at certain times when the library services guarantees to offer specific staff to help young people deal with their school, project and home-work. Staff are there to help young people help themselves to find, understand, interpret and use information and resources held in the library, or accessible via the library. They can operate every night, or once a week, depending on need and, more likely, resources.

Library staff have always helped young people find information and resources – but so many young people need far more than this. They need someone else with time, knowledge and commitment to sit with them and help – not *do*, but *help* – for as long as it takes. Library staff are seldom able to do this – homework help clubs offer a potential solution.

Homework centres or clubs often need additional resources, particularly for the GCSE level, and this may often require negotiation with the adult library as to whether this stock should be removed from the adult non-fiction and shelved separately in a homework section. Equally crucial is the access to a wide range and sufficient quantity of CD-ROMs and word-processing facilities.

Adequate staffing is what will make these clubs or centres effective. They are an additional resource, and as such can not be built on existing staffing. There is a debate as to whether this staffing should consist of teachers, librarians or youth workers. In fact all have useful skills and a combination is the best approach. Some clubs and centres are building on a mix of professional expertise, both paid and voluntary, and this works well. While librarians do have the skills to handle information, other people have deeper knowledge about some subjects or more expertise of working with the age group.

A mix of staff encourages cross-service working, and promotes the view that libraries are open to all. This is not a diminution of a librarian's work, but an extension, especially as we must remember the aim – to enhance educational achievement for young people. In Southwark, Knowsley and Northamptonshire different staffing approaches have been taken, all with excellent results. Whatever the approach, staff need to be trained, they need to have worked with young people, and need to be aware of their concerns, of changes in education and of the wider implications of using libraries. Other issues to be considered are

- opening times: after school, weekends and holidays all need to be considered
- sponsorship
- links to schools
- the relationship between books and CD-ROMs
- refreshments and toilet facilities
- charges such as photocopying, printing from the PC, etc.

Evaluation of the effectiveness of the centres or clubs is essential. This should include: measurement of any increase in skills level and educational attainment; documentation from homework projects (along similar lines to OFSTED judging the effective use of resources in schools); and increase in membership of the library, and increase in issues and enquiries. This may also be a valuable opportunity to develop qualitative measures by asking parents, young people and teachers from local schools what impact they feel the centres have had. Westminster City Libraries asked pupils what they liked about the homework club. Comments included: 'get help with homework; help when stuck; the way it is organized; library is always tidy and clean; gives you a better education; computers to help; a good peaceful place to work; you can work with and meet friends; it is great; it is brilliant'. However, some found it too noisy and crowded. Teachers meanwhile noted, in children attending the club, improvements in research skills and writing and reading, a greater accuracy in homework and an increased confidence in using the library.

Quantitative measures are also valuable. David Murray suggests evaluation of: who is attending, what age and gender they are and, if agreeable, their ethnic background; what stock the young people use most; what their most asked questions are; and what stock gaps have been identified (i.e. where was demand either not met or where was there insufficient material to meet all the requests).

References

1   Mark, J., *Thunder and lightnings*, Harmondsworth, Puffin, 1976.
2   Abbott, J., *Learning makes sense: recreating education for a changing future*, Letchworth, Education 2000, 1994.
3   Martyn, J., Twenty years on, *Information UK*, British Library, 10 October 1994.
4   The Library Association, *Curriculum guidance: National Curriculum and effective learning*, London, The Library Association, 1996.
5   Department of National Heritage, *Investing in children: the future of library services for children and young* people, London, HMSO, 1996.
6   Murray, D., *Homework help clubs*, an ASCEL briefing paper, unpublished, 1996.

10
Working together

The children's library was disguised as a big living room with pictures on the walls, and a carpet and canvas bean bags, big enough to sit on, in case people got frightened by seeing so many books, and went away again without reading anything.

J. Mark, *The dead letter box*[1]

When children are not in school, they are in the greater community. Only 20% of a child's time is spent in the classroom. The greater community is often where a child develops a sense of direction and self-esteem. Changes in education suggest that libraries have a big opportunity here, and that the opportunity for working closely with children is even greater in the greater community. One of our problems, as children's librarians, paradoxically, is our professionalism – even more pronounced in education – but we do try to be a standalone discipline rather than an integral part of a greater endeavour. We then define the discipline narrowly and happily burden it with our own rules and theories. In the past we have been rather paranoid, rather protectionist. There was an explanation – the profession was under attack, or it thought it was, from other sectors of librarianship, for a range of reasons. Such action, however, does not sit well with our professional ethic of going to some incredible lengths to obtain answers for users. Another indication that children's librarianship has changed is that within many authorities it is the children's service which is leading the way in developing partnerships.

Budgets are not infinite, and no government is promising to square the circle, so we have to look elsewhere for resources if we are going to achieve what we want. As librarians, we have failed to sell the library concept to politicians and policymakers, so working in partnership with agencies and other departments is vital. Where it has been tried, there has been much success. Some examples of this are:

Section 19[2] This is a result of the Children Act, and requires authorities to create a summary of day care opportunities for children. Many have created a children's plan as a result. Whatever the approach there should be at least a paragraph, a page – but why not a chapter in the next revision?

Bookstart Social services and health authorities may allocate budget money to libraries to run Bookstart. In Hertfordshire they have also funded a video and a multilingual leaflet. Sunderland won the Holt Jackson Community Award which has helped to make Bookstart a national success. Birmingham's research proves the worth of such initiatives.

Health As a spin-off from Bookstart, libraries have begun to work closely with health agencies, and this has led to nominations in the National Health Awards.

Early years Education and social services departments are working together with libraries in some authorities to create better access to information for the early years.

Youth work Work with young people and youth workers to develop better services, often jointly funded or supported by external agencies such as Business Link.

Europe European funding is vital to support initiatives in the future. Lancashire have gained EU money to extend their Lancashire County Council/National Westminster Bank Children's Book of the Year Award, for example, into Europe.

Business Work with business has enabled the development of homework centres, sponsored IT, provided Internet connections and supported general developments.

All this is happening now, and there are many other examples not included here. To develop joint working practices, a children's service must know exactly what it is trying to achieve. Using the business techniques outlined at the beginning of this book, the service will already be very aware of its aims and objectives, its purpose, values and goals. These are fundamental when laying the foundations of working together with other agencies.

Investing in children[3] recommended strongly the development of an integrated strategy for library provision to children. This strategy should concentrate on the integration of library provision within the school, the school library service and the public library. There is also the need for a much broader integrated strategy between all agencies working with children. The creation of a formal document is not the recommendation here. Too much time would be lost in attempting to bring together people with such a wide range of interests across such a wide age and needs group, let alone in agreeing a set of words which would not either become a strait-jacket or were too weak to have an impact. It is better to concentrate on action. With its purpose, aims and objectives, goals and values understood, the library service will have a strong backbone and it will be able to go out and seek partners who share similar objectives.

Children's librarians are now taking up important places on local youth or early years forums alongside teachers, voluntary bodies, youth workers, members of the churches and young people themselves. For some it has been a struggle to be accepted, while others may feel that, in relation to the needs of other agencies, the needs of libraries are minor. It is important to understand, however, that libraries have an important role often in unlocking opportunities for other agencies, which gives them a significant value to others. Working in this way helped Hertfordshire to develop a youth information strategy. Health promotion, the careers information service, Business Link, the police and other agencies within the authority were all identified as having an interest in youth information. All were invited to join a steering group which has proved very successful in developing an information strategy for young people, along the lines of 'A young people's information strategy' (page 103).

The output of work from such partnerships should not form the type of integrated strategy the LISC report *Investing in children*[3] refers to, although it may be a useful first exercise, but a joint strategy for improvement, development or implementation of a service.

References

1   Mark, J., *The dead letter box*, Harmondsworth, Puffin, 1982.
2   Section 19 of the Children Act 1989, which requires authorities to make a statement every three years on day care provision within the authority.

3   Department of National Heritage, *Investing in children: the future of library services for children and young people*, London, HMSO, 1996.

Part 4
The future

11
The future

Throughout the world the interest of politicians is focused on children. They are a growing proportion of our population and therefore a growing priority. Meanwhile, many feel that the industry of the next 20 years is information technology. In children's librarianship this gives us the opportunity to combine the two futures to form a focus, and to develop strong, exciting, relevant and respected provision for children and young people.

Never before has the future been so bright for children's librarianship and many feel that within our reach is the creation of a library service fundamental to the lives of young people. We have had the golden years of children's literature and they were seen by many as the glory days. They were, and we are right to remember them fondly but, looking forward, we can provide a more rounded service. Libraries will provide not just good literature but good skill development and, even more importantly, recognition by industry, business and government that they are vital to their country's future.

In many areas of work the focus is now on equality of opportunity, greater responsiveness to the community, community involvement in decision-making and greater quality of life. These themes offer opportunities for libraries to reinvent or repackage their service. They offer the opportunity to raise issues and questions, particularly in relation to previous service cuts or policy decisions. In other words, if managed properly, they could help libraries to manage themselves out of the current crisis and into a positive, more understood position.

The delegation of the schools library service is a good case in point. Such services have often struggled as a result of a reduction in budget, owing to schools using their budget for other priorities. This has had a knock-on effect on the public library service. Not only has there been ruthless use of public library resources in some cases, but this has affected the ability of young children to develop skills. Where schools have reduced their use of schools library service staff in teaching information handling skills, public libraries are consequently finding that their users need more staff-intensive help.

An argument against delegation which has much more weight, however, is the fundamental effect that it has upon the equal opportunities available to our children. If schools do not buy back the schools library service, are they not reducing children's opportunity to learn to read from a range of up-to-date and relevant resources? Should not every school be required to provide a basic minimum of reading material for its children? This is an extremely important issue in the literacy debate. In the United Kingdom, OFSTED reports are uncovering vast reductions in school book spending. This argument is very strong as it clearly cuts across current policies.

The aims of many current agendas are reflected in many topical issues, most of which the library service could use to its advantage:

Parenting is a major issue for society. As the public library review identifies

> . . . the next century will probably be a time when more than one out of every four children is born to an unmarried woman; more than two out of every three children under the age of six has a mother who is employed outside the home; fewer than three out of every ten adolescents will have lived in a continuously intact family through all 18 years of their youth.[1]

These factors present great challenges. What is needed is a dynamic, evolving service to parents or carers, including information on parenting and childcare, and provision of stability through a welcoming place and the right materials. This is seen as a new concern by some, but has, in fact, been supported by a large number of libraries for many years through their parents' collections. The Centre for the Child in Birmingham has taken this to its logical conclusion by working closely with social services to create a parents' information room within the library. There is an urgent need to achieve recognition for parenting collections before they are reinvented and 'owned' by education services. The thought of individual schools all buying a small collection is a frightening one, as each collection will age rapidly and become increasingly irrelevant as needs change. A library service, either through the schools library service or through public provision, could provide an authority-wide, circulating, viable and constantly relevant collection which would attract sponsorship and raise the profile of libraries.

Information for life choices, an area in which the children's service has been slow to see its role, is now beginning to take off. Information provision for parents on the National Curriculum and for children and young people on their rights, needs and wants, is all part of equality of opportunity and improving quality of life for individuals. It allows greater life choices, another recurring theme of the moment. It will gain support and finance because these needs are seen as fundamental to society's infrastructure.

Homework, again, is a component of the topical debate on young people. The need to support a child's homework has, in fact, been a topic in libraries for many years, but the introduction of the concept of homework centres and clubs is an opportunity not to be missed. Funding, support and recognition is suddenly available for an activity we have been doing, at least in part, for years. It gives us the opportunity to expand provision and create a better support service to children. It is vital that we obtain the staffing, the bookfund and the marketing to promote and maintain these clubs effectively.

Literacy is another area attracting initiatives from many quarters. Some of these have very little to do with reading skills. What is needed is a clear infrastructure for literacy rather than a great many independent initiatives, although if these were linked to such an infrastructure they could be very effective. Libraries could play a major role here in uniting our efforts.

Information technology is here to stay and libraries can use it to provide equality of opportunity and improve the value of life for disadvantaged users. Because of their perceived neutrality as a safe place, libraries are an ideal site for IT. Provision closes the gap between the information rich and the information poor, and allows a larger number of people to experience the very leading edge of developments.

Access As Alec Williams, Head of Children's Services, Leeds Library and Information Service, says:

> Young children have a combination of fierce inquisitiveness, boundless optimism, and vulnerability. In *their* world, anything can happen. We need to continually remind ourselves of that vulnerability, of the exploitation it attracts, and the formative role that the pleasure, the fun, the enjoyment of books can play in children's development. '*The future creeps in on tiny feet. Increasingly on impoverished tiny feet*' says the *Public Library Review*. It is becoming more and more important that all children retain easy access to libraries, and find in them that '*neutral ground between home and school,*

for independent and unhindered discovery' described by the Library Association's Guidelines.[2]

Education in the next decade is difficult to predict with certainty. What is certain is that the nature of education is changing – evolving. The view that non-competitive small group discussion, rather than class and exam-based drilling, is more suited both to the way in which our minds actually work, and to the working environment into which tomorrow's children are going is gaining weight. In some parts of the United States, technologically-advantaged families own homes overflowing with technology – fax, PC, a range of CD-ROMs, easy Internet access – which satisfies nearly all of their children's educational needs, to such an extent that some parents are only requesting school attendance for collective activities such as sports.

At the same time Bill Gates of Microsoft sees libraries as a smart way to subsidize public access to information, because the investment benefits a community of people – and on a completely even-handed basis. The future of public libraries depends on the future of:

- children
- local and national government
- publishing in all its forms
- other providers of services for children
- business and industry.

We need to be aware of the changing agendas of each of these groups, and continually repackage and develop our services to match. Libraries have been doing some excellent things for many years, often unsung, and their value and relevance often not understood. That of course is partly our fault. We now have the opportunity to attract attention to our work, make the links for the opinion-formers and the paymasters and take our services on to a new plane.

If we do not do this, then we are laying ourselves open to more budget cuts, many of whose outcomes will be insidious in their effect upon the young: the curtailment of opening hours; the withdrawal of study times; the closure of small libraries, hitting the less mobile pre-school child; the removal of magazines, which attracted teenagers; and the introduction everywhere of fines and request charges, contrary to *Investing in children*'s vision of a future service which is 'untrammelled by barriers of access such as charging?".[3]

A willingness to move with the agendas, and to repack and re-present what we do in terms of what value it can add to an agenda, is a cynical approach to some. It is, however, one way to survive and to become so vital to business, government and the local community that they not only want us to survive but to grow as well. Funding from Europe is already a possibility for European countries. European programmes such as Socrates, Leonardo, Media, Raphael and Kaleidoscope each have potential relevance; a pilot scheme about the Ariane programme is currently offering opportunities for collaborative projects on reading development; the Telematics programme already has projects with a children's dimension; and initiatives like the 'Web for Schools' project are supporting Internet development in schools throughout Europe. In some countries the lottery can fund children's initiatives and imaginative IT bids are amongst the ones most likely to succeed.

We must look to all opportunities to develop the library service in the future. Funding skills need grasping, political developments need interpreting for the library perspective, and local community issues are vital to make the service relevant to the users. We need to share and learn from each other, as together we can raise the profile of the library service to children.

References

1   Association for Information Management, *The review of the public library service in England and Wales*, London, Aslib, 1995.

2   Association of Senior Children's and Education Librarians, Conference, 1996.

3   Department of National Heritage, *Investing in children: the future of library services for children and young people*, London, HMSO, 1996.

12
Conclusion

The future of the children's service depends on many things, not least the state of local and central government and the state of publishing. But it is the state of librarianship and the position of children which matter most. The publication *Investing in children* marked a watershed in children's services. It sets a variety of challenges such as:

- providing an integrated strategy
- working in partnership
- literacy
- IT and information
- standards and specifications
- statistics
- children's charters
- status.

This also gives us huge opportunities, opportunities, in fact, to reinvent the service to young people, to use our ever-diminishing budgets creatively, to be flexible and more all-inclusive. Some may feel that we need to focus on the detail, take each recommendation in turn, be cautious with limited resources. However, there is a different way, and it begins with celebrating what we are actually doing already to 'invest in children'.

As the Comedia report says:

> The underlying principle of the public library as creating an accessible realm of knowledge remains at the heart of the reorganization of information and the public realm. But the public library service remains trapped in old forms of organization – the buildings, professional hierarchy and its current relationship with local government. In order to be the service stations on the information highway of the future, public libraries need to re-establish their basis as a resource for individuals.

We need to grasp opportunity, have the determination to drive through our plans, and to have the imagination to win what is needed for the community, our partners and ourselves. We need to anticipate tomorrow's problems, innovate tomorrow's solutions and prevent problems rather than try to sort them out too late.

Do we want a future of illiterate, uninformed people? Opportunities to learn for some but not for all: the chance to enjoy reading – if you can pay? The chance to access information – if you can pay? Without public libraries there will be no safe place, no access to all points of view, no neutral ground, no place that is local and free, no place where everyone is welcome. *Investing in children* gives us the building blocks for future library provision. What this book has tried to do is to draw the plan to identify our purpose, our values, the behaviours we need, the tasks we need to carry out and the strategies we need to complete them, and the evaluation we need to undertake in order to understand the value we need to add.

In summary, the book describes the potential of a children's service of the future, identifying the key constituent parts to enable us to maintain our status symbol of thinking and freedom. We must keep it simple, keep it short, keep it focused on the audience and above all keep it smart. When we do, we will know that we have achieved libraries where young people get a great deal every time.

Appendix
Unsupervised children in libraries: guidance notes

These guidance notes have been produced as a response to concern expressed by library staff as to their responsibilities for young children who have been left on library premises without parental supervision. It is not intended to cover all aspects of a librarian's duties towards library users. In particular it does not cover all aspects of Health and Safety legislation and fire regulations.

Introduction

Children's Libraries are designed to be welcoming places for children. Library materials are available for the children and library staff are on hand to help the children select books. Furniture and decor are often chosen to create a child-centred environment. However it is never the intention that young children should be left unsupervised by their parents or guardians.

There is a great deal of anecdotal evidence to suggest that occasionally parents misuse the facilities provided in children's libraries by leaving young children unsupervised. This may happen when the parent goes shopping though there have been cases of the library being used as a substitute for day care provision.

Libraries are public buildings to which anyone has access. Unfortunately there are in our society some people who wish to do harm to children. These people often go to great lengths to abduct children and children's libraries would be an obvious target. These guidelines have been produced to protect children and to help library staff working with children.

The legal background

Much of this section is based on *Law for librarians* by McLeod and Cooling. (Library Association: 1990). However nothing in this document should be taken as authoritative legal advice.

There exists in law the concept of a 'common duty of care' by which the occupier of premises has a duty to see that a 'visitor will be reasonably safe in using the premises for the purpose for which he is invited or permitted by the occupier to be there'.

McLeod and Cooling go on to state that 'when children are lawful visitors, the law expects additional care to be taken by an occupier on their behalf.'

The book also refers to a case of *Phipps v Rochester Corporation* (1955) in which it was held that an occupier will not always be liable for children's accidents, particularly if he could reasonably have assumed that the child would be accompanied by an adult or an older child. This relates to a case where a five year old child fell into a trench on a building site. The judge said:

> '. . . the responsibility for the safety of little children must rest primarily on the parents; it is their duty to see that such children are not allowed to wander about by themselves . . . it would not be socially desirable if parents were, as a matter of course, able to shift the burden of looking after their children off their own shoulders.'

> However, [the book continues], the judge did conclude that different considerations might apply to public places where parents might expect their children to be reasonably safe. Clearly, a public library could be such a place.

Library staff would not normally be in loco parentis (i.e. taking the responsibility of a parent). This would arise, however, if library staff accepted responsibility for a child handed over by a parent or if parents were invited to believe that library staff would look after their children.

Notes for guidance

Librarians must take 'reasonable' care of children on their premises. However there are practical limits to this care and the librarian must therefore draw the attention of parents or guardians to these limits. It should be made clear that young children should not be left unsupervised in the library. Notices should be displayed which must be of adequate size and be prominently positioned. They should be in foreign languages if necessary.

All library staff should be made aware that they should not normally accept responsibility for children. Staff should be made aware of the possibility of children being left unsupervised and there should be a clear procedure for dealing with this. This should involve a senior member of the library staff speaking to the parent or guardian. There should be a procedure for dealing with repeated cases and for special situations e.g. an unsupervised child at closing time. The principle contained in the Children Act 1989 that the welfare of the child is paramount should be born in mind. The procedures should be designed not only to remove the problem from the library but if necessary to alert the relevant authorities if the child's welfare is believed to be at risk.

Staff should also have clear instructions for dealing with adults whose behaviour may be suspicious. Obviously this calls for extreme tact and caution but warning signs must not be overlooked.

When designing a children's section in a library, provision should be made for adults who are supervising their children.

By taking these steps a library can limit its liability towards users. More to the point it can help to ensure that children using the library are not put at risk.

Organized events
Under the provisions of the Children Act, 1989 activities of less than two hours per day do not count as day care and therefore the library does not have to register under the act. In addition where day care for children is provided on particular premises on less than six days in a year, that provision does not have to be registered providing that the local authority has been notified in advance.

The library should take all reasonable action to ensure the safety and comfort of children attending organized activities. Publicity should make clear that parents should bring their children and collect them at the end of the event. The start and finishing times should be clear and kept to. The wording of notices should make it clear if the library is not accepting responsibility for the children.

Regulations in the Children Act about the number of staff and the size of groups do not apply to most library activities (see above). For example a ratio of one member of staff per eight children under eight is given (para 20c). It can be argued that this is much too restrictive for the sort of activities that take place in children's libraries. Libraries should set a reasonable limit on the number of children attending an event related to the number of adults available to supervise. It is advisable that the performer at such events (e.g. a storyteller, even if they are a member of staff) should not be counted as a supervising adult.

Professional Practice Department
and the Youth Libraries Group
The Library Association
7 Ridgmount Street
London WC1E 7AE
Tel: 0171 636 7543
Fax: 0171 436 7218

The Library Association 1991
This publication may be copied in whole or in part without prior permission, provided due acknowledgement is given.

The Library Association
Unsupervised children in libraries: Guidance notes
Checklist

- Authorities should make clear their procedures for dealing with unsupervised children. They should be laid out in a recognized document so that staff have clearly defined guidelines to follow.

GENERAL

- Library staff need to take reasonable care of all children on their premises.
- This does not absolve parents from all their responsibilities. The library must to make it clear that young children in libraries are the responsibility of parents who should accompany their children to the library and stay with them until they have made their selection.
- A notice to this effect should be displayed prominently in the library.
- Senior members of staff should be instructed in how to deal with parents who deliberately leave young children unsupervised in the library.
- There should be instructions for dealing with special situations e.g. unsupervised children on the premises at closing time.
- There should be clear instructions for dealing with people in the library whose behaviour is suspicious.

ORGANIZED ACTIVITIES

- Librarians with responsibility for children's activities must make themselves aware of their responsibilities under the Children Act and other legislation.
- Publicity for organized activities should make it clear that children should be brought to, and collected from, any activity by their parents.
- If library staff are accepting responsibility for young children for the duration of an event the starting and finishing times should be clearly stated and kept to.
- Numbers attending should be controlled e.g. by the issue of tickets and related to the number of adults available to supervise. A count of participants should be made at the beginning and end of each session.

Index